Screenwriting Workbook

The Step-by-Step Guide To Writing a Hollywood Style Screenplay

D.C. Rahe

2nd Edition

Acknowledgments

I would like to thank all those who helped me in my career and supported my writing: my brothers, John, Stephen, Paul, and Gary; my children Cameron and Elizabeth; my friends, Joe B., David R., Mark S., Jeff S., Shawn J., Sean S., Susan G., and many more.

Forward

As a writer, I have had many teachers, each having their approach to the work. Coupled with my experience, I have written this workbook that guides the novice writer by writing their first screenplay, using the Hollywood structure that producers expect to read.

According to Robert McKee, "Structure is a selection of events from the characters' life stories that are composed into a strategic sequence to arouse specific emotions and to express a specific view of life." And from William Goldman, my favorite writer, "Nobody knows anything… Not one person in the entire motion picture field knows for a certainty what's going to work. Every time out, it's a guess and, if you're lucky, an educated one."

A great idea can become a great screenplay. I have written twenty screenplays. In 2016, two of them were produced as feature films "Justice" (Universal) and "Victory Force."

Bonus

At the end of this workbook, there is breakdown of the movie "Justice:"

- Pitch

- Character Profiles

- Outline

- Screenplay

Introduction

The goal of this workbook is to finish your first draft. Forget about the idea that you are going to finish. Just write, only if it is just one page a day. Write freely and as rapidly as possible. Never correct, do not stop until you have finished the first draft. After you complete the first draft, then the hard work of editing and rewriting begins. Which is 90% of the process. Have good friends read your drafts; their feedback can be insightful.

First, read the entire workbook to become familiar with its lessons. This workbook has a straightforward approach. However, this workbook is more than just fill in the blanks. It requires reading and preparation before beginning writing your first screenplay.

This workbook takes a step-by-step approach to teaching screenwriting. We begin with a story and how to tell your story to your friends, family, and a producer. The second step is getting to know your characters and what motives them. The third is setting the location and mood. Fourth is the most important structure. The fifth is the dialogue, which convenes your story to the audience. The sixth is the formatting. And seventh is editing. Finally is the rewrite, where most of the formal writing occurs. Each step can take one to two months. Your first screenplay might take twelve months to get to the first draft. Take your time.

This workbook reviews the essential concepts mentioned in other screenwriting books regarding the story, characters, setting, and structure.

This workbook is based on the ideas of many teachers. To achieve the best results from this workbook, you must first read these screenwriting books; *Story* by Robert McKee, *The Foundations of Screenwriting* by Syd Field, *Screenwriting Is Storytelling* by Kate Wright, and *Save The Cat* by Blake Snyder. These books will give you the foundation for understanding the screenplay structure.

This workbook guides you through the step-by-step process of writing a 90 page feature-length Hollywood style screenplay. The first audience for your screenplay is a professional script reader employed by the producer, who may purchase your screenplay. You are writing a screenplay, not the shooting script. So, no camera angles. You intend to write the story that a director will interpret into a shooting script, which will produce the actual movie.

This is your workbook. I encourage you to write in it. You will need a pen and legal pads to write your screenplay.

The pen icon is a reminder that it is best to handwrite your notes and screenplay on paper. Writing by hand, you feel the paper, and you direct movements with your thoughts. Most of all, the process slows the brain down to think of the big picture. (National Pen)

"Write freely and as rapidly as possible, just get it down. Never correct or rewrite while writing your first draft, do not stop until you are finished. Rewriting while writing will only impede your progress."
- John Steinbeck

Lesson 1:
Your Story

What's your story? You have to discover your story before you begin the screenplay. This workbook is based on the premise that you already have a story idea. This workbook will guide you through the process of taking that idea and forming it into a screenplay.

To begin you need to focus your idea into a story. What will you tell your friends about your story. Develop a short pitch with the following structure.

What's the title: *Justice*

When: *1870's*

Where: *Arizona territories*

Who: *US Marshall discovers his brother is murdered by group of outlaws.*

Put these elements together to tell your story in a short pitch.

It's the 1870's a U.S. Marshall comes to a small frontier town of the Arizona territories, where he discovers that his Preacher brother has been murdered. He meets a Young Widow who provides insight to what is happening in the town. The story concludes with the Young Widow and US Marshall getting justice for the townspeople.

Exercise 1

1. Story title:

2. When:

3. Where:

4. Who:

5. Put it together in a paragraph, two or more to explain your story idea:

Congratulations, you have completed your first lesson. You are now on your way to writing your first screenplay.

"The story...must be a conflict, and specifically, a conflict between the forces of good and evil within a single person."
- Maxwell Anderson

Lesson 2:
Story Conflict

Above all, the story must have conflict. From the Greeks, we have four types of disputes.

- Hero versus Villain, external struggle

- Hero versus Nature, external struggle

- Hero versus Society, external struggle

- Hero versus Self, internal struggle

A good story has more than one of these conflicts; however, there must be one major conflict above all others.

Exercise 2

From the four types of conflict choose one for your story and explain why:

Notes

The play's the thing.
- William Shakespeare

Lesson 3:
Story Arcs

The hero must face challenges. These are the best emotional story arcs.

- **Hero wins at the end:** The hero struggles but wins in the future, i.e., *Aladdin*.

- **Rags to riches:** A steady, ongoing rise in emotional valence, with only minor setbacks.

- **Man in a hole**: The life sucks arc. Hero appears to be spiraling downward, then has a sudden success.

- **Cinderella:** Hero has early success suddenly all is lost, then turns it around for success.

- **Hero loses at the end:** The villain beats the hero. *Casablanca*

- **Tragedy or Riches to rags:** An ongoing fall emotional, or tragedy such as *Romeo and Juliet*.

- **Icarus:** Everything is going great for the hero than he fails.

- **Oedipus:** Hero can't catch a break, then has a success than fails in the end.

Exercise 3

What is your story arc and why?

Notes

"The script is the most important element in the whole process. You can have flaws in a film and still get away with it if the script is strong, but if you have a weak script, it doesn't matter how good everything else is."
- Frank Darabont

Lesson 4:
Story Types

Another way to describe your movie besides just a genre is by type. Here are Blake Synder's list of movie types:

- Monster In The House
- Golden Fleece
- Out Of The Bottle
- Dude With A Problem
- Rites Of Passage
- Buddy Love
- Why Did It Happen
- The Fool Triumphant
- Institutionalized
- Superhero
- More Types
- Fish Out Of Water
- Big Fish In A Small Pond

Exercise 4

What is your story type and why?

Notes

"Forget about the idea that you are going to finish. Just write, only if it is just one page a day. Just start writing."
- John Steinbeck

Lesson 5:
Story Genres

Your first screenplay must use a known genre; Action, Comedy, Crime, Drama, Experimental, Fantasy, Historical, Horror, Romance, Science-fiction, Thriller and Western.

Many genres have sub-genres. Know and study all the genres to find the one that is the best fit for your story.

- **Action:** the hero must endure many physical and violent encounters that can be life or death. James Bond, Jason Bourne, "Fast and Furious."

- **Action comedy:** Comedy that emphasizes physically humorous antics, unorthodox body-language and often exasperating situations. "Princess Bride", "Shazam!"

- **Adventure:** this is the action movie that takes place in exotic locations and historical time periods. Indiana Jones, Jack Sparrow.

- **Comedy:** get the audience to laugh. It can be physical, emotional and intelligent jokes and situations. Sub-genres; action comedy, comedy-drama, mockumentary, rom-com, and satire. "Long Shot"

- **Comedy-drama (dramedy):** It balances the heaviness of drama against the lightness of comedy. "Jo Jo Rabbit"

-

- **Crime:** this includes police and legal procedures, courtroom dramas and detective stories. It's all about committing the crime, or solving it, or prosecuting it. "Ocean's 11"

- **Drama:** the situation and characters take life seriously. Sub-genres; medical, legal, philosophical, psychological and political. "Joker"

- **Docudrama:** are the based on a real event story, that is dramatized for entertainment. "Sully"

- **Experimental (Art House):** do not waste your time with this genre. Typically these stories do not follow the Hollywood structure thus producers and agents are not interested. These are usually self-made films for festival audiences, and do not make a profit.

- **Fantasy:** fantastic, magical, supernatural forces, mythological or folklore in exotic worlds. Harry Potter

- **Historical:** often period pieces that may or may not be based on actual events or characters. Most genres can fit inside history dramas. "Downton Abbey"

- **Horror:** these stories scare the audience. It can be an extreme version of a Fantasy that has gone too far. "Friday The 13th"

- **Mockumentary:** it may appear as a documentary but turns the subject on its head, by making fun of the situation and characters. "This Is Spinal Tap"

- **Musical:** similar to a RomCom, but the actors sing their dialogue. "La La Land"

- **Romantic comedy (aka Rom-com):** Get two people to fall in love. "Crazy Rich Asians"

- **Satire:** it makes fun of society, institutions, governments, companies and people who take themselves too seriously. "Borat"

- **Science fiction:** take science theory and make it science fact in the future. "Star Trek"

- **Teen drama:** that awkward time when transitioning from child to adult. "Twilight"

- **Thriller:** similar to horror, instead of an ugly monster, it's a regular human that is going to kill. "A Quite Place"

- **Western:** set in dusty towns and ranches of the 1870s American West using stock characters, cowboys, gunslingers, and bounty hunters. Good guys in white hats, and bad in black hats. "Justice"

Exercise 5

What is your story genre and why?

Notes

"And by the way, everything in life is writable about if you have the outgoing guts to do it, and the imagination to improvise. The worst enemy to creativity is self-doubt."
- Sylvia Plath

Lesson 6:
Characters

Characters are born; they are real. They must grow by showing their arc as they reach their goals toward the end. Every emotion must gain in strength; every decision must become graver, every event more fascinating. In this respect, each element in the story must strengthen the character. The strengthening of characterization and emotion should come gradually, without undue jumps. The characters invent their reality; therefore, any circumstances that happen to the hero are circumstances brought on herself because of their worldviews.

It's easy to find characters because they are all around you. People are a mix of many types and traits influenced by their parents, family, environment, education, experience, and friends. The following is a list of different character types and traits. Your character should be a mix of at least two types and traits.

Character Types

Reformer

Health conscience, rational, idealistic, principled, purposeful, self-controlled, and perfectionistic.

Helper

Caring, interpersonal, generous, demonstrative, people-pleasing, possessive, and desire to feel love.

Motivator

Success-oriented, pragmatic type, adaptable, excelling, driven, and image-conscious.

Romantic

Sensitive, introspective, expressive, dramatic, self-absorbed, temperamental, self-aware, sensitive, and reserved.

Thinker

Intense, cerebral types, perceptive, innovative, secretive, isolated, alert, insightful, and curious.

Skeptic

Engaging, responsible, anxious, suspicious, committed, security-oriented, reliable, hard-working, accountable, and trustworthy.

Enthusiast

Spontaneous, extroverted, optimistic, versatile, acquisitive, and scattered.

Leader

Strong, powerful, dominating, confident, decisive, willful, aggressive, resourceful, ego-centric and domineering.

Peacemaker

Easygoing, self-effacing, reassuring agreeable, and complacent

Character Traits

Humility

Humble, modest, reverence, altruism, pride, modest behavior, selflessness, and giving respect.

Patience

Resolve conflicts and injustice peacefully, and create a sense of peaceful stability and community.

Diligence

A strong work ethic, steadfast, fortitude, conviction, integrity, and the capability of not giving up.

Chastity

Cleanliness through cultivated good health and hygiene, and maintained by refraining from intoxicants, with moral wholesomeness.

Kindness

Positive, cheerful, empathic, trust, compassion, unselfish love and voluntary kindness.

Temperance

Mindfulness, self-control, abstention, moderation, deferred gratification.

Charity

Benevolence, generosity, sacrifice, and self-sacrifice.

Loving

Unlimited loving-kindness, ultimate perfection of the human spirit, and self-sacrificial.

Lustful

Passion, sexual desire with appetite for money, fame, or power.

Gluttonous

Selfishness, over-indulgence and over-consumption of anything to the point of waste.

Greedy

Disloyal, betray, treason, bribe, steal, trick, manipulation and violence.

Lazy

Do nothing for oneself or others.

Angry

Self-destructive, violent, hateful, inordinate and uncontrolled feelings.

Envious

Jealous when comparing oneself to others.

Prideful

Hubris, self-importance, and excessive love of self.

Creating the character

To create a character, you must combine character types of traits that make sense of the story. Always be with your hero. Who is he? What is his background? Why does he do what he does?

How does your hero motivate your story? Is the villain is as important as the hero to the story? Get to know all your main characters. What are their motives? All characters have an equal chance for their goals to succeed.

The audience must have empathy for the storyline as told by the characters. Your story must have characters that an audience can identify with favorably, that they can have sympathy for them. All character names MUST be different, spelling, and sounding. Every hero needs a sidekick, confidant, or mirror, and a villain. How similar and different are these characters in their relationship with the hero?

Hero

Is an idealistic, conformist, face incredible odds, face conflict bravely, they are motivated by pure intentions, is good looking, always gets the love interest, extraordinary, talent, on the right side of the law, pro-active, deceive, conventional morals, achieves goals, wants to overcome his flaws, and find his real purpose and destiny, learns a lesson, and in the end is changed for the better.

Villains

Is a realist, a rebel, independent, comforts authority, uses sneaky strategies, driven by basic urges, usual looks, no love interest, no unique talents, idiosyncratic moral compass, manipulates the law, passive, pushed into situations, swears, drinks, casual sex, drug user, failure, mysterious, unpredictable, selfish, self-centered, unchanged.

Main Characters

The audience must know the following about all the main characters (hero, sidekick, villain, henchman): Character name, age, social-economic environment, culture, type, traits, education, health, occupation, goals, sub-goals, relationships, opposite, overlapping goals, character traits, appearance, personality, emotions, mannerisms, expressions, conflicts, and surprises.

Example Character Profile

Hero name: James McCord

Age: Mid-thirties

Social-economic: middle class, war veteran

Culture: Religious family

Type: Leader

Traits: Diligence, charity, temperance

Education: 10th grade

Health: Excellent

Occupation: Lawman, US Marshall

Goals and Sub-goals: Revenge brother's murder, end corruption

Relationships: Befriends Melissa and her family

Opposite of Mayor Pierce, Reb

Overlapping goals with Melissa

Appearance: Tall, great physical shape

Personality: Serious and determined

Emotions: Minimal

Mannerisms: Courteous, simple

Expressions: Blank, no smile

Conflicts: Duty for law and his family

Surprises: Quotes bible verses

Exercise 6

Create a detailed profile for each of your main
characters, Hero, Sidekick, Villain, Henchman, then add the
most essential supporting characters as necessary.

Name:

Age:

Social-economic:

Culture:

Type:

Traits:

Education:

Health:

Occupation:

Goals and Sub-goals:

Relationships:

Opposite of character name:

Overlapping goals with character name:

Appearance:

Personality:

Emotions:

Mannerisms:

Expressions:

Conflicts:

Surprises:

Notes

"A successful book is not made of what is in it, but what is left out of it."
- Mark Twain

Lesson 7: Setting

Location

On the first page, the audience must know where the story is taking place. Set the stage for the audience. The place is a crucial element of the story.

Beyond the slug line, the scene heading gives a general description of its place, so it becomes familiar to the audience. The location is a powerful influence on the characters. Is this a familiar or unfamiliar place?

Time

When in time does the story take place? I would suggest setting now, in a contemporary time. The past has too many facts, and the future is unreal. Even when flashback scenes have are used, the characters need a contemporary time that fits their story. Flashbacks are a trap that novice writers MUST avoid. Keep the timeline moving forward; going back and forth confuses the audience.

Exercise 7

Describe the following of your story:

Atmosphere:

Time period:

Locations:

Notes

"Every story should have a beginning, a middle, and an end."
- Peter De Vries

Lesson 8:
Structure

Since the Greeks, plays have been divided into three acts: a beginning, a middle, and an end. A play begins by introducing the location and characters, followed by the conflict, which must be resolved in the conclusion.

A good structure clearly defines the main plot, the hero's journey, and the subplots that support or block the hero. Subplots, even without the hero present, are used to fill-in the details of the story.

Within every scene, there must be conflict. Every character in every scene has their own goals, their own agenda to succeed in that scene. That's the conflict.

Once you have completed your structure, then you'll need to provide more detail using scenes. Each scene comprises a single dramatic action, there is a Set up, a Confrontation, and a Resolution.

This book guides you through writing your screenplay using the hero's journey structure. However, there are other types of structures you should become familiar with as a screenwriter.

The following are five ways to outline a screenplay: by Hero's Journey, by Acts, by Steps, by Beats, by Sequences and by Plot Points.

Hero's journey, is the ancient storyteller's structure, with many steps along the journey to success. Go to page 113 for more detail.

Acts, is the traditional playwright's structure of three acts of beginning, middle and end.

Steps, is the step-by-step approach.

Beats, is the modern method of structuring the screenplay with various beats of the story.

Sequences, is the most logic method of structure.

Plot Points is the easiest and fastest method. It is as easy as filling in the blanks.

Structure Types

Hero's Journey

Act One: The Departure

1.   Status quo

2.   The call to adventure

3.   Refusal of the call

4.   Meets mentor

5.   Crossing the threshold

6.   Belly of the whale

Act Two: The Initiation

1.   The road of trials & tests

2.   The meeting with the goddess

3.   Woman as temptress

4.   Atonement with the father

5.   Apotheosis

6.   The ultimate boon

Act Three: The Return

1.   Refusal of the return

2.   The magic flight

3.   Rescue from without

4.   The crossing of the return threshold

5.   Master of two worlds

6.   Freedom to live

7.   New status quo

Acts

Act One: The Setup

1.   Where and when is this story happening?

2.   What are the hero's and villain's goals? Should conflict.

3.   Who are the support characters?

4.   How do supporting characters help the hero and villain achieve their goals?

Act Two: The Challenge

1.   Show the hero's steps to reaching his goal against the
      villain's counter goal.

2.   At the middle, events become more dangerous.

3.   The counter goals become more sinister, the hero's
      goal and villain's goal have equal chance of
      succeeding.

4.   Each scene must give new information, which
      confirms or denounces the previous information.

5.   Follow the interest, and develop anticipation.

6.   Forward movement: new sub-goal starts before
      previous sub-goal has been satisfied or frustrated.
      Each sub-goal must be in accordance with the main
      goal. Steadily increase audience's interest and raise
      their feelings of suspense.

7.   Audience anticipates of a certain happening. The
      event occurs as anticipated - fulfilled expectancy.

8.   Audience anticipates of a certain happening.

9.   Shock the audience. End the Act with a scene that is
      unexpected.

Act Three: The Conclusion

1.   Is the resolution logical?

2.   It is believable?

3.   It is clearly stated?

4.   Have I left any questions unanswered?

Steps

Act One: The Beginning

1.   Hook - opening scene sets time and location

2.   Set Up - characters set goals

3.   Inciting Event - Turning point that calls to adventure

4.   Build Up - Tension ramps up conflict

5.   1st Plot Point - Key plot event

Act Two: The Middle

1.   Reaction - Hero scrambles to villain obstacles

2.   1st Pinch Point - Villain wins, reveals nature of conflict

3.   Realization - Hero becomes informed and grows

4.   Midpoint - Hero realizes central truth of the conflict

5.   Action - Hero makes headway against Villain

6.   2nd Pinch Point - reminds Hero whats at stake

7.   Renewed Push - Hero has small victory.

Act Three: The End

1.   3rd Plot Point - Hero's reversal of fortune

2.   Recovery - Hero questions choices

3.   Climax Begins - Hero confronts Villain

4.   Confrontation - Duel with winner take all

5.   Climactic Moment - Hero achieves goal

6.   Resolution - Final emotional climax

Beats

1.   Opening Image

2.   Theme Stated

3.   Set-up

4.   Catalyst

5.   Debate

6.   Break into Two

7.   Subplot

8.   Fun and Games

9.   Midpoint

10. Bad Guys Close In

11. All is Lost

12. Dark Night of the Soul

13. Break into Three

14. Finale

15. Final Image

Sequences

Sequence 1 - Intro hero, motives, story premise, time, tone, location.

Sequence 2 - Introduce villain, motives, goals.

Sequence 3 - Hero reluctant to take on new goal.

Sequence 4 - Hero goes on adventure to achieve goal.

Sequence 5 - Hero is pushed back by the Villain's achievements.

Sequence 6 - Hero confronts the Villain.

Sequence 7 - Hero struggles and fails against the Villain.

Sequence 8 - Villain now controls the storyline.

Sequence 9 - Hero defeated physically and mentally by Villain.

Sequence 10 - Hero gives up.

Sequence 11 - Hero gathers strength and courage to face Villain.

Sequence 12 - Hero is the winner.

Plot Points

1. This is a modified version of the Hero's Journey with other structure types.

2. Hook/Image: Start in the middle of a mess to hook audience fast.

3. Setup: Introduce characters and show what is normal.

4. Enter Villain: Big entrance showing what they do best.

5. Supporting Characters: Reveal different sides of the story.

6. Plot Goal: Problem arises along with first plot goal.

7. Goal Defined: Hero must change accomplish plot goal.

8. Gauntlet: Reveal antagonist goals.

9. First Test: Hero may fail to show weakness.

10. Inciting Incident: Event happens that changes what is normal.

11. Exile: Hero leaves familiar world to accomplish plot goal.

12. Plot Goals Restated: New plot goal worth leaving home?

13. Theme Goals Restated: Use metaphors or fable.

14. Unforeseen event pushes plot forward.

15. Investigation: Hero fumbles around in dark to do plot goal.

16. Meet Mentor: Teacher, wizard, godlike force.

17. Acquire New Tools: New skills, tools or information

18. Joke: Funny moment to relieve tension.

19. Foreshadow: Prepare audience for surprise ending.

20. Unique Genre Element.

21. First Theme Success: Show small character arc and
     growth change.

22. Triumph First Plot Success: 1st plot goal
     accomplished.

23. Betrayal: Supporting characters or hero own
     weakness.

24. Big Bad Twist: Unexpected turn of events with new
     plot goal.

25. Torture/Escape: Hero suffers then saved by new skills.

26. Defeat: Hero loses previous win with added suffering.

27. Reassess Plot Goal: New plot goal direction
     evaluated.

28. Restate Theme Goal: Film theme or character arc
     growth.

29. Mentor Disabled: Hero goes forward alone.

30. Second Joke: Funny or playful moment.

31. Unique Genre Element.

32. Surrender: Hero gives up in face of impossible odds.

33. Unexpected event moves plot forward.

34. New Solution: Unexpected solution is discovered.

35. Final Confrontation: Fight brewing between
     characters occurs.

36. Death: Hero defeated along with supporting
     characters.

37. Resurrection: Strength gathered for another
     confrontation.

38. Sacrifice: Arm lost, choice over lover or loot.

39. Revelation: Show protagonist epiphany related to
     theme.

40. Climax: Protagonist wins in moment of greatest
     intensity.

41. Resolution: Who lives/dies, gets the girl/guy,
     celebration.

Exercise 8A

Fill out the structure of your story. After each number write one to five words for each scene.

1.   Hook:

2.   Setup/Enter Hero:

3.   Enter Villain:

4.   Enter Supporting:

5.   Plot Goal:

6.   Goal Defined:

7.   Gauntlet:

8.   First Test:

9.   Inciting Incident:

10. Exile:

11. Plot Goals Restated:

12. Theme Goals Restated:

13. Unforeseen event:

14. Investigation:

15. Meet Mentor:

16. Acquire New Tools:

17. Joke:

18. Foreshadow:

19. Unique Genre Element.

20. First Theme Success:

21. Triumph First Plot Success:

22. Betrayal:

23. Torture/Escape:

24. Defeat:

25. Reassess Plot Goal:

26. Restate Theme Goal:

27. Mentor Disabled:

28. Second Joke:

29. Unique Genre Element.

30. Surrender:

31. Unexpected event:

32. New Solution:

33. Final Confrontation:

34. Death:

35. Resurrection:

36. Sacrifice:

37. Revelation:

38. Climax:

39. Conclusion:

Exercise 8B

Having completed the plot structure, now you need to write the scene structure. Write an action sentence for each part of the scene, set up, confrontation, and resolution. Begin each scene with a slug line, INT. for interior, EXT. for exterior, and I/E. for both, example:

INT. SUSAN'S BEDROOM - NIGHT

Hook

Slug line

Setup

Confrontation

Resolution

Hero enters

Slug line

Setup

Confrontation

Resolution

Villain enters

Slug line

Setup

Confrontation

Resolution

Supporting enters

Slug line

Setup

Confrontation

Resolution

Plot Goal

Slug line

 Setup

Confrontation

Resolution

Goal Defined

Slug line

Setup

Confrontation

Resolution

Gauntlet

Slug line

Setup

Confrontation

Resolution

First Test

Slug line

Setup

Confrontation

Resolution

Inciting Incident

Slug line

Setup

Confrontation

Resolution

Exile

Slug line

Setup

Confrontation

Resolution

Plot Goals Restated

Slug line

Setup

Confrontation

Resolution

Unforeseen event

Slug line

Setup

Confrontation

Resolution

Investigation

Slug line

Setup

Confrontation

Resolution

Meet Mentor

Slug line

Setup

Confrontation

Resolution

Acquire New Tools

Slug line

Setup

Confrontation

Resolution

Joke

Slug line

Setup

Confrontation

Resolution

Foreshadow

Slug line

Setup

Confrontation

Resolution

Unique Genre Element

Slug line

Setup

Confrontation

Resolution

First Success

Slug line

Setup

Confrontation

Resolution

Celebrate

Slug line

Setup

Confrontation

Resolution

Betrayal

Slug line

Setup

Confrontation

Resolution

Torture/Escape

Slug line

Setup

Confrontation

Resolution

Defeat

Slug line

Setup

Confrontation

Resolution

Reassess Plot Goal

Slug line

Setup

Confrontation

Resolution

Restate Theme Goal

Slug line

Setup

Confrontation

Resolution

Mentor Disabled

Slug line

Setup

Confrontation

Resolution

Second Joke

Slug line

Setup

Confrontation

Resolution

Unique Genre Element

Slug line

Setup

Confrontation

Resolution

Surrender

Slug line

Setup

Confrontation

Resolution

Unexpected event

Slug line

Setup

Confrontation

Resolution

New Solution

Slug line

Setup

Confrontation

Resolution

Final Confrontation

Slug line

Setup

Confrontation

Resolution

Death

Slug line

Setup

Confrontation

Resolution

Resurrection

Slug line

Setup

Confrontation

Resolution

Sacrifice

Slug line

Setup

Confrontation

Resolution

Revelation

Slug line

Setup

Confrontation

Resolution

Climax

Slug line

Setup

Confrontation

Resolution

Conclusion

Slug line

Setup

Confrontation

Resolution

Notes

"All the information you need can be given in dialogue."
- Elmore Leonard

Lesson 9: Dialogue

The best writers are excellent observers of life; they listen carefully to everyone around them. Before your characters speak, you must know them. Live with your feelings for a while; wait for them to talk to you and listen. Each character has their voice, vocabulary, usage, manner and pattern. Be sure to include cultural, education and class or social status. It must be unique. Your characters will lead you to your story. Just follow them.

To write dialogue, you must first study dialogue. If you are writing a drama, listen to your favorite movie drama, do not watch it. Frequently stop it at each scene. Listen to how the story and characters are revealed through dialogue and actions. Listen to how subtly and continuously the plot unfolds until all factors are exposed. Listen for the contrasts and conflicts and how decisions are made. Listen to how characters cut each other off to express their ideas.

Exercise 9

Now that you have completed the second outline of your screenplay, you are ready to write dialogue for your characters. The dialogue explains to the audience each character's situation and motivations.

You are now leaving the outline format behind and using the correct screenplay format described and show in the next lesson on Formatting. Each page represents one minute of running time for the movie.

This exercise takes time and many pages to write. It gets you closer to a screenplay.

Using the correct format, get out your pen and legal pad and begin writing your screenplay.

Notes

"If you are stuck on a scene, skip it and move onto the next scene. When you finish, you can go back and complete any holes in your story."
- John Steinbeck

Lesson 10:
Formatting

Most published scripts in books or archives are of a movie's shooting script, not the original screenplay that was submitted. Your screenplay should have these characteristics: no scene numbers, very few camera shots, and sequences written in master scenes. Do and Don'ts.

1.   No camera directions

2.   No opening credits

3.   Only 'fade in' and 'fade out.' No 'cut to,' 'dissolve,' etc.

4.   Capitalize character names

5.   At least 90 pages, no longer than 120 pages

6.   Dialog no longer than five lines

7.   Scenes no longer than five pages in length

8.   Scene descriptions are no longer than four lines

9.   Character names should sound differently. Start character names with different letters.

10. Minor characters do not need names

11.   Slugline: INT. SUSAN'S BEDROOM - NIGHT

12.   Use Courier 12-point, ten-pitch, non-proportional

13.   Printed on white bond paper, 20 lb.

Screenplay standard format, white paper, page size 8.5 x 11 inches, font Courier, 12 pt. The top margin is one inch (1"), the dialogue margin begins at three inches (3") and ends at six point two inches (6.2"). The description and slug line margin starts at one point seven inches (1.7") and ends at seven point five inches (7.5"). Scene headings (slug line) are always ALL CAP with INT. for interior, EXT. for the exterior, and I/E. for when a scene goes in and out of a building. There is one single space break between the slug line and the description. The bottom margin is usually one inch (1").

The following two pages are examples of correct screenplay format.

```
                        "Title"

                      Written by

                    Author Name




          Agency Name (if applicable)

          123 Main Street

          2nd Line (if Needed)

          Anytown, ST 99999

          (999) 555-1212

          emailaddress@yourdomain.com
```

FADE IN:

EXT.   VERY FIRST SLUG - DAY

This is Action style after First Slug,
which is only 2X spaced after FADE IN:
above. USER, new character names are
always ALL CAPS.

                    CHARACTER NAME
                 (parenthetical)
               Dialogue.

Back to Action after viewing CHARACTER,
PARENTHETICAL, and DIALOGUE styles.

INT. CLASSROOM - NIGHT

The students sit waiting for the bell
to ring, STUDENT#1 seats next to
STUDENT#2.

                    STUDENT#1
                 (Digusted)
               You stink.

                    STUDENT#2
                 (Irritated)
               No, you do.

                    STUDENT#1
                 (Angry)
               Shut up!

Student#1 slaps Student#2 in the face.
Fists start flying.

FADE OUT.

The End

"A good writer is not someone who knows how to write, but how to rewrite."
- William Goldman

Lesson 11:
Editing

Again, congratulations, you have completed your first rough draft of your screenplay. You have come a long way to get to this point. Now, the rough part, having someone you trust read your first draft. But, before you do, proofread it for the following.

- Typos/misspelling on the title page

- Typos/misspelling in the first scene header

- Typos/misspellings in the first sentence or paragraph or page

- Triple/double spacing of every/many lines (s) on first page

- Lack of spacing between scene header and description and/or between description and dialogue and/or between dialogue and dialogue

- Use of font other than Courier 12-point, ten-pitch, non-proportional

- Use of bold print

- Dialogue that stretches from the left margin to the right margin

- Extra space between character name and dialogue

- Description and/or dialogue typed ALL CAPS

- Extremely narrow or extremely wide outside margins

- Long, long, long descriptive passages

- Handwritten or hand-printed screenplays

- Other glaring, non-standard format usage

Avoid Mistakes

The fewer the mistakes, the greater chance that your screenplay will be read.

Printing

Today most screenplays are sent as PDFs. But in the case that a printed screenplay is required, here are guidelines for a professional-looking printed 90 pages and no more than 120 pages screenplay.

MUST:

- Print on white bond paper in the correct format

- Front and back covers on subdued colored card stock

- Front cover has Title only

- Three-hole punched

- Two brass brads

AVOID:

- Art on the cover

- Hard, slick covers (with long metal connectors)

- Bright color card stock cover

- Commercial, "college paper" covers

- Permanent binding (i.e., plastic spine binding)

- ○ Wimpy brads

- ○ Long "dangerous" brads, cut "dangerous" brads

- ○ A "clipped" or "rubber-banded" screenplay on non-three hole paper

- ○ Double-sided printing

- ○ Too thick or too thin. Three-ring binding

Exercise 11

Now take your handwritten screenplay and type it into a word processing program. Check it for spelling, punctuation and grammar. Print it. Next have someone you trust and respect read it.

Notes

"Writing isn't about making money, getting famous, getting dates, getting laid, or making friends. In the end, it's about enriching the lives of those who will read your work, and enriching your own life, as well. It's about getting up, getting well, and getting over. Getting happy, okay? Getting happy."
- Stephen King

Lesson 12:
Rewrites

You have spent one year of your life writing your first screenplay. During this time, you have learned a great deal about how people communicate and your view of the world. Now comes the actual work—the rewrites.

After you have had people read your screenplay. Listen carefully to their comments. Their emotional reaction to your story is more important than their words about the story. Because your story is about feelings you want for a reaction, that's the point of movies.

Exercise 12

Read your screenplay from start to finish. Reread it. Take your notes, your friend's notes, now begin the rewrite. In this part of the process, you'll tighten the story; you'll smooth the edges as if you are sanding a piece of wood.

After each draft, have more people read it. Keep smoothing the rough edges. Once you have gotten to the best screenplay that you can write, now you need actors. Schedule a table read with an actor for each part; when you hear them speak your screenplay, that's when it comes alive.

Now enter your polished screenplay into writing contests. You'll receive professional feedback, but it gets in front of producers who are seeking the next great movie.

Good luck.

Notes

"Be careful of falling in love with a particular scene. It might not work when the entire screenplay is finished."
- John Steinbeck

Lesson 13:
Pitch

Explain your story utilizing the seven elements of storytelling to writing your pitch. I have included one of my movies as an example.

- **Title:** (kept it short, less than four words): Justice

- **Genre:** Western

- **Type:** Dude with a Problem

- **Pitch:** (it's a hit movie combined with another hit movie): 3:10 to Yuma meets True Grit.

- **Story:** (one or two sentences, less than 20 words): "US Marshall avenges the murder of his preacher younger brother in the Old West."

- **Synopsis:** (4 paragraphs, 1 for each Act)

  - Summary of the entire story

  - Act 1 - Setup:

  - Act 2 - Confrontation:

  - Act 3 - Resolution:

- **Outline:** Scene by scene breakdown.

- **Treatment**: (optional)

A narrative telling of your story is over twenty pages, similar to a short story. Each page is a story beat. I don't recommend this step. I would rather give the producer a detailed outline.

Exercise 13

Mastering these story elements will help you pitch your story from the simplest to the more complex.

Title:

Genre:

Type:

Pitch:

Story: Synopsis:

Summary:

Act 1 - Setup:

Act 2 - Confrontation:

Act 3 - Resolution

"First, find out what your hero wants,
then just follow him!"
- Ray Bradbury

Appendix A: Hero's Journey

Your story must have a structure. The best first screenplay to use the story structure of the hero's journey (Joseph Campbell). A hero is the story. The hero can be female, male, non-binary, or an animal. A chronicle of the hero's growth is the story structure. The events in the screenplay will happen due to who the characters are, what circumstances on the outside affect the hero on the inside.

From page one, you must capture the audience's attention with a fantastic event, but not so big of an event that overshadows subsequent larger events. Give the audience a rest period just after the middle section. Each event rises in importance and intensity, leaving increasingly shorter rest periods until we reach a quick and high-intensity end.

Each element of the story must rise while having the highest point at the end. The end of each Act is a significant twist. Some conditions changed, showing new information, thus the story changes direction.

Joseph Campbell analyzed many ancient stories and developed this theory of storytelling. That every significant story is a Hero's Journey told in 17 steps.

1.   **The Call:** The hero is told about an adventure.

2.   **Refusal Of The Call:** The hero refuses to go because of a sense of duty or fear, or insecurity.

3.   **Meeting The Mentor:** Once the hero has committed to the quest, a mentor will be his guide.

4. **Crossing The Threshold:** The hero leaves behinds his world and venturing into an unknown and dangerous realm.

5. **Belly Of The Whale:** The hero faces a setback then is willing to undergo a metamorphosis.

6. **The Road Of Trials:** The hero faces tests and failures. Eventually, the hero will overcome these trials and move on to the next step.

7. **Meeting The Goddess:** This is the ultimate test of the hero's talent to win the boon of love, which is life itself enjoyed as the encasement of eternity.

8. **The Temptress:** the hero faces those temptations, often of a physical or pleasurable nature, that may lead him to abandon or stray from his quest.

9. **Atonement:** the hero must confront whoever holds the ultimate power in his life. This is the center point of the journey.

10. **Apotheosis:** the hero discovers a greater understanding.Now the hero must be ready for the toughest part of the adventure.

11. **The Ultimate Reward:** is the achievement of why the hero went on the journey to get.

12. **Refusal Of The Return:** Having found bliss and enlightenment in the other world, the hero may not want to return to the ordinary world.

13. **The Magic Flight:** The hero must escape with the reward. It can be just as adventurous and dangerous, returning from the journey to go on it.

14. **Rescue From Without:** The hero must have powerful guides and rescuers to bring them back to everyday life.

15. **Crossing The Return Threshold:** The trick in returning is to keep the wisdom gained on the quest, and to share the knowledge with the rest of the world.

16. **Master Of Two Worlds:** At this step, the hero may achieve a balance between the material and spiritual. The person has become comfortable and competent in both the inner and outer worlds.

17. **Freedom To Live:** Mastery leads to freedom from the fear of death, which is the freedom to live. We sometimes refer this to as living in the moment, neither expecting the future nor regretting the past.

Appendix B: Sources

Screenplay: The Foundations of Screenwriting by Syd Field

Story by Robert McKee

Save The Cat by Blake Synder

Screenwriting Is Storytelling by Kate Wright

The Power of Myth by Joseph Campbell

Letters *from John Steinbeck,* Edited by Elaine Steinbeck and Robert Wallsten

Writing Screenplays That Sell by Michael Hauge

From Reel To Deal by Dov S-S Simens

40 Plot Points For A Feature Film By Sherri Sheridan

Handwriting by National Pen

Screenplay Format by Greg Beal, Motion Picture Academy of Arts and Sciences,

Writer's Guild of America/West

The Writer's Circle Magazine

Wikipedia

Notes

Bonus:
Movie Breakdown

All good stories have a back story. Prior to being asked to rewrite the "Justice" screenplay, I had established good personal relationships with the co-writers.

Shawn Justice, is a filmmaker who writers, directs and produces independent Christian movies. He is a fine man and father, who has deep Christian faith. I have a great respect for him and his valves. I am always happy to work with him.

Jeff Seats is an artist. Known in the theatre community as a set designer. A man with an expert eye for detail. He has written a novel too. We always have great conversions. I believe we have a mutual respect.

Shawn come up with the idea for "Justice" had written up a rough outline, which he give to Jeff to write the first draft of the screenplay. Once that was completed, Jeff asked me to punch up the characters and dialogue and tighten up the structure. After I was done, Shawn completed the preacher's scriptures. We submitted the screenplay to the producers.

The producers were thrilled by the screenplay. On its merits, they raised the money to produce the movie. When the director was hired, he contracted an additional writer to turn the screenplay into a shooting script. A few scenes were added, and they changed the location from the Pacific Northwest to New Mexico. The completed motion picture, "Justice" was released by Universal Pictures in 2017.

The following is the breakdown for the "Justice" movie, pitch, story elements, character profiles, outline and screenplay.

NOTE: The name of a new character are always ALL CAPS. Screenplays do not have camera angles and no "CUT TO:" Special note on location, the original "Justice" screenplay was written for the Pacific Northwest The movie was produced in New Mexico, the shooting script was written to fit the new location. Many scene locations will be different.

To fit the screenplay into this book's printed page, the format has changed, as well as the font size and the margins reduced. The correct format is white paper 8.5 x 11, Courier 12-point, ten-pitch, non-proportional. One minute per page.

Movie Pitch

The pitch is a progressive process that captures a producer's imagination. The process slowly reveals the story elements, beginning with the title. It must be short and to the point. Second is the type of story, followed by a short and succinct sentence that tells the entire story. If the producer is interested, they might request a synopsis. One one to two pages that includes four paragraphs, a summary paragraph, followed by the setup, the confrontation and the resolution paragraphs.

This pitch conveys the traditional Western genre story of a good guy, a US Marshall who is seeking justice for the murder of his younger brother set in the 1870s in frontier town. The visual of every Western made before it with its deserts, rolling hills, wide open skies, cowboys, settlers, townspeople and bad guys. "Justice" is a traditional Western that was produced in the United States during the 1950s and early 1960s. This era of moviemaking and style of screenplay influenced the screenwriters of "Justice" writing.

Even in this new millennium, there are audience members you yearn for simple stories of good and evil. This screenplay includes bible verses and references that depict a moral code to follow that these audience members find reassuring. As a writer, it is good to know your audience.

Movie Elements

Title: *Justice*

Type of story: Dude with a Problem

Pitch: It's *3:10 to Yuma* meets *True Grit.*

Story: US Marshall avenges the murder of his preacher younger brother in the Old West."

Characters:

- James McCord (hero)
- Thomas McCord (teacher)
- Mayor Pierce (villain)
- Melissa Green (sidekick)
- Reb (henchman)

The following are the character descriptions for each of the major characters.

Hero name: James McCord

Age: Mid-30's

Social-economic: middle class, war veteran

Culture: religious family

Type: Leader

Traits: knowledgeable, clear, mindful

Education: 10th grade

Health: Excellent

Occupation: Lawman, US Marshall

Goals and Sub-goals: Revenge brother's murder, end corruption

Relationships: befriends Melissa, and her family

Opposite of: Mayor Pierce, Reb

Overlapping goals with: Melissa

Appearance: Tall, great physical shape

Personality: serious and determined

Emotions: minimal

Mannerisms: courteous, simple

Expressions: blank, no smile

Conflicts: Duty for law and his family

Surprises: speaks bible versus

Teacher/Mentor name: Thomas McCord

Age: Late-20's

Social-economic: middle class

Culture: religious family

Type: Reformer

Traits: knowledgeable, clear, mindful

Education: Harvard Divinity School

Health: Excellent

Occupation: Preacher

Goals and Sub-goals: Save souls, end corruption

Relationships: befriends Melissa, and her family

Opposite of: Mayor Pierce, Reb

Overlapping goals with: Melissa

Appearance: medium, great physical shape

Personality: serious and determined

Emotions: passionate

Mannerisms: courteous, simple

Expressions: stern

Conflicts: Serve God, or myself

Surprises: defiles Mayor Pierce

Villain name: Mayor Pierce

Age: 50's

Social-economic: middle class, war veteran

Culture: farmer's

Education: 12th grade

Health: Good, smokes cigars

Occupation: Mayor, entrepreneur

Goals and Sub-goals: power, money, Melissa

Relationships: boss of Reb and henchmen

Opposite of: James McCord

Overlapping goals with: Reb

Traits: knowledgeable, clear, mindful

Appearance: Fine, well-groomed

Personality: serious and determined

Emotions: controlled passion

Mannerisms: direct

Expressions: no smile

Conflicts: the past

Surprises: distrusts everyone

Sidekick: Melissa

Age: 30's

Social-economic: low

Culture: religious family

Education: 6th grade

Health: Excellent

Occupation: farmer

Goals and Sub-goals: keep congregation together, fight Pierce and support James

Relationships: mother and father, and James

Opposite of: Mayor Pierce

Overlapping goals with James

Traits: listens, devout Christian, seeks justice

Appearance: plain, well-groomed

Personality:compassionate and determined

Emotions: caring, sincere

Mannerisms: simple

Expressions: cheerful, determined

Conflicts:dangers of Pierce and henchmen

Surprises: her attraction to James

Henchman: Reb

Age: 30's

Social-economic: very low

Culture: criminal

Education: 1st grade

Health: poor

Occupation: gun slinger

Goals and Sub-goals: greed, lust, power

Relationships: supports boss, Mayor Pierce

Opposite of: James

Overlapping goals with Pierce

Traits: shoots first, reacts

Appearance: dirty

Personality: rough, unfeeling

Emotions: exterior

Mannerisms: simple

Expressions: unsmiling, uncaring

Conflicts: James, the law

Surprises: rapist

Notes

Movie Outline

Justice

INT. CHURCH - NIGHT

1870 - Fort Howard

REVEREND THOMAS McCORD, late thirties, clean-shaven, neat and tidy, wears glasses, writing in his journal.

The very sexy prostitute, GINNY POST, sets him up.

Thomas is beaten unconscious by the Mayor's Henchmen, BUFORD, WHITEY, LEFTY, SLIM, and REB.

Reb lights the church on fire.

EXT. CHURCH - NIGHT

Reb, Buford, Lefty, Slim, and Whitey exit the church as it bursts into flames.

MAYOR RICHARD PIERCE fifty-year-old stern, strong face watches the church burn.

EXT. FORT HOWARD GATE - DAY

JAMES McCORD, rough-looking dark-haired 40-year-old, rides a horse through the old fort's gates turned into a town.

James releases a black teenager from
being whipped by Slim.

INT. SALOON - DAY

James asks the BARTENDER, a fifty-year-
old man, for directions to the church.

Reb, Whitey, and Buford sit at the
table playing cards.

James announces he's looking for his
brother, Thomas McCord.

Buford asks what to do. Reb replays
play cards.

INT. MAYOR'S HOUSE - DAY

The Mayor cleans his Lefaucheux
revolver.

Reb listens. The Mayor talks of his
plans without any inference from the
Preacher, his brother, or anyone else.

EXT. BURNED CHURCH - DAY

James looks through the ruins. Only the
large wooden cross remains standing.

MELISSA GREEN COLLINS, late twenties,
direct and straightforward, wears a
gold band on her left-hand meets,
James.

EXT. GRAVEYARD - DAY

James collapses on his knees. He hands
Thomas's letter to Melissa.

She reads it aloud. Then we hear Thomas
reading the letter. She discovers that
James is a US Marshall.

INT. CHURCH - MORNING

FLASHBACK SCENE Thomas delivers a
sermon condemning the town's
corruption.

Reb and Henchmen witness the sermon.

EXT. BURNED CHURCH - DAY

Melissa tells James that Thomas was
killed the night of his sermon about
the town's corruption.

Melissa invites James to stay in their
old cabin.

James and Melissa ride his horse. She
tells him of her husband, who died in
the war, and her son died of
diphtheria.

INT. GREEN'S HOUSE - EVENING

James meets Melissa's mother ELIZABETH
GREEN, 50s, and her father, STRATTON
GREEN 50s, in their modest and small
house.

James tells them of his relationship
with Thomas and about their contrasting
personalities.

Stratton and Elizabeth give their
impressions of Thomas.

EXT. GREEN'S HOUSE - DAY

FLASHBACK SCENE

Thomas sits in a group of men,
Elizabeth brings more food. He
compliments her.

Stratton warns Thomas about the Mayor.
Thomas believes that he must stand up
to the Mayor.

INT. GREEN'S HOUSE - EVENING

Melissa tells James she was told he was
drunk and dropped the oil lamp. James
knows that Thomas would not get drunk

Stratton agrees no one had ever seen
Thomas drunk.

Melissa states was a kind Thomas man
who believed any soul could be saved.

Stratton provides Mayor Pierce's
backstory.

EXT. GREEN'S HOUSE - PORCH - NIGHT

James and Stratton sit drinking
whiskey.

Stratton smokes his pipe. He goes on
about Thomas's good character.

Melissa gives Thomas's tin box to
James. He opens it to reveal some
papers and a blurred photo of two boys.

James talks about the photo. He is sad.

He removes his mother's gold ring and
hands it to Melissa. She's embarrassed,
he continues and removes Thomas's
journal book.

Melissa hands the ring back to James
and says goodnight.

INT. BEDROOM - LATER - NIGHT

James lights a lantern and sits on the
edge of a cot. As he reads Thomas's
diary, Thomas's voice is heard.

Thomas tells of his destiny to teach
the word of God. Then he goes into
detail about the corruption.

Thomas found a stockpile of weapons. He
drew a map in the journal.

After he spoke up, he was attacked by
the Mayor's Henchmen.

Thomas was interested in Melissa.

INT. BLACKSMITH SHOP -DAY

Buford and Whitey are harassing the blacksmith, SOLOMON WASHINGTON, Large Black man, 40s. Buford holds Solomon's hand near the fire.

James into the shop with his gun drawn.

James hits Buford's wrist, holding Solomon with the butt of the gun handle. Buford lets out a shriek and let's go.

Buford and Whitey exit.

INT. SALOON - DAY

James walks into the saloon filled with Townspeople, Soldiers, Reb, Buford, Whitey, Slim, Lefty, and Ginny.

At the bar, James orders two drinks.

Reb gives James the evil eye. The Townspeople act nervous.

James sits down with US Army CAPTAIN LEWIS, man, 30s, and puts the drink in front of him.

James asks for the Army's help. The Captain turns him down.

They speak of their experiences during
the war.

Captain Lewis provides Reb's
background.

After the second round of drinks, the
Captain that he might if the situation
is dire.

INT. TOWN STORE - LATER - DAY

Buford is shaking down MRS. TRIMBLE,
woman, 40s, the proprietor. While
Whitey is breaking items.

James enters and pulls his gun and
cocks the hammer. Whitey and Buford
turn at the sound.

Buford nods to Whitey, who sets the
item down, and they take a step back
from the counter. Buford explains that
he's here to collect the rent.

Buford gives Whitey a nod, and they
turn to leave. He stops at the door and
addresses Mrs. Trimble that the
Marshall won't be around forever.

EXT. MAYORS HOUSE - PORCH - DAY

The Mayor sits at a small table sipping
coffee. Reb, Buford, and Whitey stand
with hats in hand.

Buford explains his troubles with James. The Mayor is not happy that the Henchmen are overreacting. Wait and see what happens.

EXT. GREEN FARM - MORNING

James on the porch watches Melissa feed the chickens.

Melissa looks up and sees James watching her. She walks to him.

James tells her that the Mayor and his Henchmen might have killed Thomas.

James shows her Thomas's coded map. He is going to check it out; if any happens, contact Captain Lewis.

EXT. FOREST - DAY

MONTAGE SCENE - James follows the map to old trappers fort

1. James rides out of town

2. James pauses to check the map.

3. James stops at a stream his horse takes a drink. He checks the map.

4. James rides through a thick forest. Ducking branches.

5.   James stops when he sees an
     overgrown structure.

I/E. TRAPPERS FORT - DAY

A small stockade almost entirely
overgrown.

James, with gun drawn, cautiously
approaches and goes inside the old
fort.

He notices crates and barrels are
stacked up next to the cabins' walls in
a very haphazard way.

He pries open a barrel and discovers
rifles. He finds casks of black powder,
dynamite, and gold coins.

EXT. GREEN'S HOUSE - DAY

James rides up and dismounts, while
Melissa is shelling peas in a large
bowl on her lap.

James tells her that he has found the
Old Trappers Fort, that it's filled
with weapons.

He rides away.

EXT. ARMY ENCAMPMENT - DAY

James informs Lewis of the cabin filled with rifles and power for a small army.

Lewis shares that the territory lawless, and he is concerned that there are Confederates such as the Mayor and his men, who may wish to claim the territory by force.

Lewis agrees to help James only if there's violence

INT. MAYORS HOUSE - PARLOR - EVENING

Mayor sits looking at his ledgers. Reb enters, pours two whiskeys, and sits down.

Reb informs the Mayor that James rode North that he didn't follow him.

The Mayor tears Reb down. He tells Reb to tell James to leave town.

EXT. BEHIND THE BUILDING - NIGHT

James exits the saloon and walks to his horse. Ginny appears and lures him to follow her.

Ginny leads James back behind the building and stops.

She tears her clothes and pretends to be raped by James.

Reb and the thugs beat James senseless,
leaving him on the ground.

EXT. BEHIND THE BUILDING - NIGHT

James lies face down in the dirt. He
wakes up in a lot of pain.

Slowly, painfully and staggers to get
on his horse.

EXT. GREENS HOUSE - NIGHT

James, in pain, crashes onto the porch
and makes a loud noise.

Stratton exits the house with his
shotgun ready. Elizabeth and Melissa
are right behind him. They see James,
beat up and in a mess on the porch, and
help him inside.

EXT. BURNED CHURCH - MORNING

The congregation has assembled facing
the sanctuary sitting on chairs from
home.

The Greens arrive in their wagon.
Melissa and Elizabeth help James down
while Stratton gets their chairs from
the wagon.

The Greens with James sits as if in the
front row.

Everyone is silent. With no preacher, Melissa stands in front.

The congregation greets her. She asks them to pray as she gives a sermon on what happened to Thomas, what James is doing, and the Mayor.

The congregation is not interested, too afraid to speak.

WILLIAM REY, 40's speaks they have too much to lose.

Solomon thanks James for helping, but he needs to think of this family first.

Mrs. Trimble also stands and thanks James, but the others are wrong. We must stand up to the Mayor.

James painfully stands says that justice for brother is his responsibility, but the Mayor's corruption is their responsibility.

The congregation stands up, take their chairs, and leave.

Melissa helps James to Thomas's grave.

EXT. THOMAS'S GRAVE - MORNING

James and Melissa come to a stop at Thomas's grave. James frees himself from Melissa's helping hand, approaches the grave and stops, and looks down at it. He says to the grave that he needs to fight.

Melissa looks into James's eyes. He shouldn't. He retorts that justice is his job. They freeze in a near embrace.

EXT. MAYOR'S HOUSE - PORCH - DAY

The Mayor sits reading *Democracy in America* by Tocqueville, trying to look intelligent.

Reb enters, casting a shadow over the Mayor. Asks about the book. Mayor replies, researching how to run a country.

Reb tells him of James's efforts to get the churchgoers to help me. The Mayor laughs it off. He orders Reb as the Sheriff to arrest James for rape of Ginny. Then he can begin his revolution.

EXT. COMMUNITY GARDEN - DAY

James and Melissa stroll hand in hand.

James provides Melissa with background about Thomas and himself.

Melissa knew Thomas was interested in her, but she did not return his affections.

Reb, Buford, Whitey, Slim, and Lefty,
with guns drawn, surround James and
Melissa.

James reaches for his gun, and Reb
stops his hand from behind, pulls it
out, and points it at James.

Reb is showing sheriff's badge, arrests
James for the rape of Ginny.

Melissa looks to James in disbelief
about the rape charges.

EXT. STREET - DAY

James is tied to the whipping post.

As Melissa watches James, the Mayor
appears behind her, talking.

Melissa is startled, turns, and faces
the Mayor.

The Mayor keeps Melissa distracted
while James is whipped.

Mayor tells her of the new start for
the territory. If she choices the
Mayor, the charges against James will
be dropped.

As Melissa turns, the Mayor grabs her
and brings her close. He smiles, making
sure that she understands his drift.

Melissa breaks his grip runs to the
bloody James.

INT. GREEN'S HOUSE - DAY

Melissa sits at a table with Stratton
and Elizabeth discussing James.The
Mayor wants James dead. Melissa says
she loves James.

EXT. FORT HOWARD - DAY

MONTAGE SCENE Stratton speaks to
members of the congregation.

1.   MOS. Stratton asks Solomon for help.
     He turns his head, no. Stratton
     pleads but no go.

2.   MOS. Stratton asks another man. He
     listens. Agrees.

3.   MOS. Stratton rides up to a man in a
     field. They talk. The man agrees.

4.   MOS. Stratton approaches a couple on
     the road. The man shakes his head,
     no.

EXT. GREEN'S HOUSE - MORNING

A group of seven congregation men with
their guns have assembled, including
Solomon and William.

Melissa tells them of the Mayor's plans
for turning the territory into his own
country and that they must break James
out of jail.

I/E. JAILHOUSE - DAY

Slim stands guard becomes attentive,
and holds his rifle at the ready.

Stratton arrives with a canvas bag for
James.

James sits in a small cell, while Lefty
sits guard with a rifle.

They can hear Stratton as he describes
each of the many food items in the bag.

Lefty unlocks it and opens it a crack
to see the stuff that Stratton has
brought.

Slim and Lefty are distracted. Stratton
glances up and sees Solomon and William
slip beside the jail door.

Stratton pulls a handgun on Slim. Lefty
attempts to slam the door shut, but
Solomon and William force their way in.

Lefty pushed up against the bars, James
grabs him.

Stratton motions for Slim to go into
the jailhouse.

EXT. MAYOR'S HOUSE - PORCH - DAY

The Mayor is sitting on his porch,
reading one of his books on democracy.
He sees Stratton pointing his gun at
Slim.

The Mayor stands in surprise.

Reb comes running Mayor tells him to
get more men.

The Mayor picks up a gun while watching
the jailhouse.

INT. JAILHOUSE - DAY

Stratton demands the key. They don't
have it Reb does.

The Solomon pulls out a hammer and
chisel. He works the cell door.

EXT. ARMY ENCAMPMENT - DAY

Melissa asks Captain Lewis for help. He
protests that it's a local matter he
has no authority over.

INT. JAILHOUSE - DAY

Solomon breaks the lock, and the door
swings open.

The Slim and Lefty are tied up and
sitting on the floor.

Stratton opens the jailhouse door, and a shot glances off the door frame. They are trapped.

James grabs the Lefty's rifle, stands by the door, ready to charge out.

EXT. ARMY ENCAMPMENT - DAY

Melissa and Captain Lewis react to the sound of gunfire coming to the town.

Captain Lewis orders his men to the town.

I/E. JAILHOUSE - DAY

When the jailhouse door opens, it is. Peppered with gunfire by Reb and a few of his Henchmen are positioned around the jailhouse.

With no escape, James ties a white towel to the barrel of the rifle.

Stratton asks why surrender. James states it's a distraction to gain time.

James smiles at Stratton, opens the door, and pokes the flag out the crack.

Reb cautiously stands, pointing his gun in the direction of the jailhouse.

James makes a slow, hesitant move out the door. Once on the porch, the door closes shut behind him. James takes several steps towards Reb.

Reb raises his rifle and aims at James.

James stares him down unafraid.

The sound of a shot rings out. James remains standing.

Reb is shot in the arm and falls to the ground. Captain Lewis with Melissa and several of his Soldiers. Captain Lewis is lowering his rifle, having just hit Reb. He orders his soldiers to round up the Henchmen.

Melissa runs to James as Stratton, Solomon, and William exit the jailhouse.

EXT. MAYORS HOUSE - PORCH - DAY

The Mayor has been watching the action from his porch. He mounts a horse and makes for an escape through the town gate.

EXT. JAILHOUSE - DAY

Melissa, James, Stratton, Solomon, and William are gathered together in a celebration of relief.

James stuffs a couple of handguns in his belt and picks up a rifle, then

climbs on a horse to ride after the
Mayor.

Melissa shows the map to Stratton,
Solomon, and William.

I/E. TRAPPERS FORT - DAY

Mayor dismounts and runs inside the
stockade.

The Mayor rushes inside to grab a
couple of loose empty bags.

James arrives, dismounts draw his gun,
and proceeds inside.

The Mayor lights a lantern,
illuminating a treasure room filled
with boxes and bags of gold coins,
paper currency, jewelry, and other
stolen treasures. He knocks over a
strong box that crashes to the ground.

James hears the crashing sound and
follows its direction, and then he
hides behind some crates.

The Mayor continues to fill his bags.

James yells at the Mayor to surrender.

Mayor stops filling the bags and draws
his gun. He looks around and sees James
crouched behind crates. He aims and
fires.

James unhurt rolls along the ground to a better firing position and returns fire.

A gunfight ensues. The Mayor is firing at James and missing while James returns fire and misses. Then the firing stops from inside the cabin.

James charges inside. While Mayor reloads.

James tackles him to the ground. Then James stands and brings his gun to bear on the Mayor.

James lowers his gun just a bit. The Mayor throws debris into James's face.

James staggers back.

The Mayor springs to his feet and grabs a bag of loot.

James grabs him and pulls him to the ground, where he proceeds to beat the stuffing out of the Mayor.

Melissa, Captain Lewis, and a squad of Soldiers arrive and dismount. Captain Lewis leads the way.

The Soldiers remain outside. Captain Lewis and Melissa follow the noise of the fight. They discover James mercilessly beating the Mayor to death with his bare hands.

Captain Lewis pulls James off the Mayor
while keeping his gun trained on the
Mayor.

Melissa pulls James to the side and
tries to calm him down.

Captain Lewis drags the Mayor out of
the cabin and stands him before James
in the open.

Mayor says diapering words about
Melissa and Thomas.

Melissa is shocked.

James pissed raises his gun at the
Mayor's head.

Mayor pleads for his life with the
Captain. It's James's call, not his.

James holds the gun inches from the
Mayor's forehead. The gun shakes in his
hand. He is ready to shoot.

Melissa places her hand on James's
shoulder, and he drops the gun to his
side, and he breaks. They hug.

With everyone's guard down, the Mayor
breaks free he runs into another cabin
and slams the door closed.

The Mayor barricades the door closed.
In the dark, he lights an oil lantern,

which reveals a room full of crates of
rifles, ammo, and gun powder.

The Mayor gets a rifle and looks out
the window.

Mayor yells out to make a deal. James
only wants Justice.

A shot rings out from the window and
nearly hits James. The three duck
behind crates.

The Mayor continues to fire. The rifle
jams, he pulls out his Lefaucheux
revolver.

Captain Lewis and James open fire into
the open window.

The spray of gunfire causes the Mayor
to fall back. He repositions himself.
He has a clear shot of James. He pulls
up his revolver with both hands in aim
it and fires.

The Lefaucheux revolver blows up in the
Mayors face. He falls back and knocks
over the light lantern, and fire
quickly spreads. He's blinded. He
staggers around, trying to wipe his
eyes clean.

The fire flares up, and the room is
fully illuminated, showing stacks of
guns and barrels of powder and crates
of TNT.

The Mayor stomps at the flames for a moment but realizes that it is a lost cause, and the fire like the sides of the barrels and crates.

The Mayor tries desperately to remove the barricade.

Mayor yells for help.

James goes to the door and tries to push it open.

The ammo begins to explode around the Mayor.

Captain Lewis pulls James away from the door.

The fire licks out the small window. The Mayor's screams for help.

A powder keg explodes, and the row of cabins is consumed in flames.

James, Melissa, and Captain Lewis flee with the horses a safe distance from the Trappers Fort.

Melissa hugs James as they watch the old fort as it explodes and burns.

James announces that's the end of insurrection. Captain Lewis agrees.

Melissa prays for the Mayor's soul as the fire consumes him.

The three mount their horses and ride
back to town.

EXT. BURNED CHURCH - AFTERNOON - DAY

James, Melissa, and Captain Lewis on
their horses have stopped at the church
ruins.

The cross foundation looks very weak.
The cross appears to be titling down
forward. They don't notice.

James dismounts.

Captain Lewis rides off.

James assists Melissa dismount. He
holds her around the waist, facing him
they look into each other eyes. They
are about to kiss.

Reb appears from behind the ruins. With
his gun drawn on them.

Before James can go for his gun.

James puts himself in front of Melissa.

Reb figures that James killed the Mayor
and claimed the loot for himself. He
wants it.

James says the Mayor died in the fire.
The authorities will recover the loot.

The cross's foundation continues to crumble. The cross tilts down toward Reb.

Reb states it's all his. He admits he killed Thomas.

Reb aims at James.

CRACK, the sizable heavy cross falls onto Reb's head. Then CRASH, Reb is crushed.

EXT. JAILHOUSE - LATE AFTERNOON - DAY

James and Melissa ride up to the jailhouse. Reb's body lays across James's horse. Captain Lewis, with Soldiers, Stratton, Solomon, William, and Towns Men, stand circling the Mayor's Henchmen, including Slim, Buford, Whitey, and Lefty are sitting on the ground.

Many of the townspeople, including Ginny, are there.

Buford stands stopped by a Soldier. Declares that James killed both the Mayor and Reb.

James states their actions got themselves killed.

The Soldier grabs Buford and sits him down.

James approaches Captain Lewis,
requesting that he watch the prisoners
until he can return with more US
Marshalls.

EXT. GRAVE - MORNING

James riding his fully loaded horse
stops at his brother's grave.

James tells his brother's grave that he
got his justice.

He hears a noise coming from behind him
and quickly turns, drawing his gun.

Melissa approaches James as he stands.
They face gazing into each other's
eyes, then embrace and kiss.

She asks what happens when he returns.
He doesn't know. She tells him the
position of Sheriff is available.

They embrace again, kiss, and embrace,
holding the moment as the camera pulls
out, as the sunsets.

FADE OUT

Notes

Movie Screenplay

FADE IN:

INT. CHURCH OFFICE - NIGHT

1870 - Fort Howard

REVEREND THOMAS McCORD, late thirties, clean shaven, neat and tidy, wears glasses, sits at his desk, bible open, his oil lamp burns, and his tin box is open. He concentrates on his writing in a leather bound journal book. Suddenly there is a KNOCK at the door.

He is surprised, nearly jumps. He looks at his watch, it's 9:10 p.m. He puts away his journal, tying it with a black ribbon, then puts it into the tin box, opens a desk draw, puts the box inside, and closes the draw.

He stands and crosses to the door, opens it to reveal a very sexy prostitute, GINNY POST. Thomas adjusts his glasses at the sight and clears his throat.

                    THOMAS
          Yes, Ginny. How can I
          help you?

She gives him a sly smile.

                    GINNY
          Can I come in? I need to
          talk.

Thomas looks around nervously.

                    THOMAS
          I'd rather you not.

Tears start to stream down her face.

                    GINNY
          Please pastor, I need to
          talk, I want to give up
          this life. I can't do it
          any more.

Thomas studies her and then opens the
door a little further.

                    THOMAS
          Okay, come in.

She enters, wiping her eyes. But as he
closes the door a sinister look is on
her face. She sits down in one of the
chairs.

Thomas walks over.

                    GINNY
          Pastor, I'm ashamed of
          who I am.

                    (pause)
          What I've become.

Thomas gives her a warm smile.

          THOMAS
      It's okay Ginny. That's
      where you need to be
      when you come to God. He
      takes that and makes
      something beautiful out
      of it.

She sniffles.

          GINNY
      Really?

Thomas puts his arm around her to
comfort her and leads her to the office
door.

          THOMAS
      Now you head on home
      Ginny. We can talk more
      about this tomorrow at a
      more... uh...appropriate
      hour, but now I think
      the both of us need to
      call it a night.

          GINNY
      Thanks reverend.

          THOMAS
      Well, I'm here for you
      and all my congregation.

Ginny gives him a slight peck on the
cheek

>   GINNY
>   Good night rev and thank
>   you
>   again.

Thomas looks around and marks his place
in the bible he was reading.

A Foot Step SOUND comes from within the
church.

He looks up and listens intently.

The sound again.

He lifts the oil lamp off of the desk
and goes out into church proper.

INT. CHURCH - NIGHT

A noise is heard from a dark corner by
the door. Rev McCord lifts his lamp up
to see what caused the clatter. He
steps close to the door. He sees
nothing but some loose papers in the
pew next to him. He sets the lantern
down and bends to tidy up the pew.

BUFORD, one of Mayor's henchmen, large
and imposing steps behind him unseen
and lifts his arm with a club in his
hand.

When Thomas straightens the club comes
down on him.

WHITEY is standing behind him, a club
in his hand that he brings down on the
back of Rev's head. Rev McCord
collapses to the floor.

From the dark corner another man steps
out into the light of the lantern. REB,
a menacing hulk of a man, dirty,
unkept, a nasty individual. He slowly
chews his tobacco, then spits it on
floor, displaying no respect for the
church or the pastor. He's flanked by
LEFTY, and SLIM, two more henchmen.

Thomas rolls over and slowly opens his
barely conscious eyes.

                    REB
          Having a little late
          night snack there
          reverend?

Thomas in the middle, Reb circles him,
they the henchmen form a circle around
both of them.

                    THOMAS
          What? What are you...

                    REB
          Ginny, you know she's my
          girl
          right rev?

Thomas rubs the back of his head.

                    THOMAS
               (surprised)
          What? No! She came to me
          for guidance.

                    REB
          That why she kissed you?

Reb kicks Thomas in the gut.

Ginny enters the church and nuzzles up
to Reb.

                    GINNY
          Thanks Thomas, I always
          wondered what it was
          like with
          a preacher man.

A confused, angry look comes across
Thomas' face.

                    THOMAS
          Now look here Ginny,
          nothing happened and you
          know it!

She gives him a pouty face.

                    GINNY
          Oh Thomas, now don't be
          sore.
               (beat)
          I like you.

With that she turns around to leave,
gives Reb a passionate kiss and exits
the church.

Thomas looks bewildered.

Reb gives Thomas another stiff kick to
the head.

                    REB
          That one was from me.

Reb kicks him one more time.

                    REB (CONT'D)
          And that one was from
          the
          Mayor.

                    REB (CONT'D)
               (beat)
          The Mayor told you to
          keep your nose out of
          his business. Warned
          you. You should've gone
          along you'd have some
          money, a new church, but
          no.

Reb nods to Whitey, who clubs the rev
again.

Reb grabs a lamp and empties out the
oil around the church interior. He
grabs the lantern by the unconscious
Thomas and lifts it up and drops it
into a pool of the oil on the floor.

                    REB
          See you on the other
          side Rev.

The interior of the church becomes
engulfed in flames as Reb LAUGHS and
his men exit.

EXT. CHURCH - DAY

Reb, Buford, Lefty, Slim, and Whitey
exit the church as it bursts into
flames.

A man stands on a nearby porch,
watching the scene. The orange of the
flames illuminates the face of MAYOR
RICHARD PIERCE. A smile grows across
his fifty year old stern and slightly
chubby face. He turns and walks into
the shadows.

EXT. GATES OF THE TOWN - DAY

Ft. Howard, an old British fort turned
into a town. It is surrounded by a
sturdy log wall. Most of the town
exists within these walls. Since the
war the army has shown up to utilize
the fort as a regional military post
for the protection of the settlers as
they move west.

A lone figure on a horse rides through
the gates. He has no purpose. No face.
Only a large Stetson hat, wearing it so
naturally. The brim casts a dark shadow

across his features. He looks to his left.

POV: Between two buildings, Lefty beats up a Black teenager.

Some of the townsfolk take no notice as they go about their daily chores. Others take note of the mysterious brooding quality he radiates as he heads his horse to the saloon. He looks to his right.

POV: Two prostitutes are hustling a Townsman.

Strangers are a common sight in the fort/town since the end of the war but not many come wearing the baggage that this one seems to be wearing. He looks ahead.

POV: A man, shirtless, blood drips from his cut up back, is strapped to a whipping post. Slim stands by with is bullwhip.

The rider dismounts, ties up his horse methodically.

The CAMERA FOCUSES on every detail of this stranger.

His guns resting at his side.

His boots kick up dust.

His Spurs.

His hat

He looks up to reveal his face, JAMES McCORD, rough looking dark haired 40 year old, with focus in his eyes.

He steps to the boardwalk and goes to the doorway and heads to the saloon door.

INT. SALOON - CONTINUOUS - DAY

James saunters through the doors of the saloon. The saloon is fairly calm at this time of day. A few people turn around to look, but it doesn't cause much of a stir.

He walks up to the makeshift bar, planks across the top of barrels. And slaps down a coin and orders a whiskey. The BARTENDER serves him, warily, and James downs the drink, slams another coin down and asks for another, the action repeats.

James turns to the Bartender.

                    JAMES
          Anyone here can tell me
          where the church is?

The room becomes deathly silent.

James looks around and sees several men
duck their heads down not wanting to
make eye contact.

                    JAMES (CONT'D)
          No one? No one knows
          where the church is?

He turns back to the bar shaking his
head.

The bar tender hesitantly steps back to
the bar.

                    BARTENDER
               (nervously)
          Anything else?

                    JAMES
          Not unless you can point
          me in the direction of
          the church, no.

The bartender gives the room a once
over glance looking for input. Seeing
none he pours himself a shot then looks
at James.

                    BARTENDER
          Down the street to the
          left.

James turns to leave.

                    BARTENDER (CONT'D)
          Not that you'll find
          much there.

James takes a step back to the bar top.
A question on his lips.

The bartender hesitates and looks at a
table full of rough looking guys. One,
Reb, gives him a "shut the hell up"
kind of look.

> BARTENDER (CONT'D)
> (nervously)
> Go back out the main
> gate and head West.
> You'll find it in the
> orchard. Can't miss it.

The bartender turns his back on James
and cleans some glasses.

James looks around the room. Reb,
Whitey, and Buford, sit around a table
playing cards. All the people are
studying the table tops, their drinks
or the cards they are holding, everyone
except for Reb. He glares at James.
James glares back. Tension fills the
room.

James turns to the room and says.

> JAMES
> If any one of you
> happens to see
> Reverend McCord please
> tell him his brother's
> in town. And, uh, thanks
> (MORE)

                    JAMES (CONT'D)
          for your help. I'd
          appreciate it.

James exits the saloon.

Reb quietly stares at James as the door
closes. The background noise starts to
rise as the men begin to relax a bit.

Buford sitting next to Reb leans in and
asks.

                    BUFORD
          What're you goin' to do
          Reb?

Reb picks up his hand of cards and
studies them.

                    REB
          Play cards. I call.

INT. MAYOR'S HOUSE - LATER - DAY

Reb walks into the Mayor's house.

Mayor sits at his kitchen table, a
cloth is spread out with the parts of
his Lefaucheux revolver nicely
organized with a small can of oil, and
a cleaning cloth. The Mayor holds the
barrel, he looks through it.

POV: Reb is framed through the barrel.

Reb crosses to the sideboard, pulls out
two glasses, uncorks the whisky
decanter and pours two drinks.

                MAYOR
        It was a tragic thing
        having to kill a man of
        the cloth.

Mayor cleans each piece as he assembles
the gun.

                REB
        You gave him plenty of
        chances. It's not your
        fault, he had to be
        killed, just like that
        last preacher man.

Reb walks over to the Mayor, places one
of the filled glasses near him.

                MAYOR
        I have a vision for this
        territory. You're either
        with us, are against us.
        Even if he's a man of
        God.

                REB
        What about his
        followers?

                    MAYOR
          They're a ship without a
          rudder.With no one to
          lead them they won't
          bother us.

                    REB
          But now that his
          brother...

                    MAYOR
          Well, you'll have to
          inform him of the
          situation here. With us,
          or against us.

                    REB
          I'm not sure. I'm
          tellin' you he's going
          to be trouble.

                    MAYOR
          And, why do you say
          that?

                    REB
          I've seen his type
          before.

Reb sips his drink.

                    REB (CONT'D)
          He's a dog with a bone.
          He's digging around.

                    MAYOR
          Doesn't he believe it
          was a tragic accident?

                    REB
          Not sure.

                    MAYOR
          Well, perhaps he may be
          from an accident prone
          family.

Reb smiles nastily.

                    REB
          Yeah, maybe he is.

                    MAYOR
          Let's wait and see how
          "clumsy" he is.

The revolver is fully assembled. The
Mayor holds it up with two hands, arms
extended, he takes aim at objects
around the room.

                    REB
          Be careful with that
          Frenchie gun. Why don't
          you get yourself a
          Colt.

                    MAYOR
          My father's revolver?
          Did you know Colt, that
          damn Yankee,
                         (MORE)

                    MAYOR (CONT'D)
          stole Lefaucheux's
          design.

                    REB
          Just be careful with it.
          They're not as reliable
          as a Colt.

                    MAYOR
          Don't worry I keep it in
          working order, and it's
          always on me.

The Mayor slides the revolver into his
front chest leather holster.

EXT. BURNED CHURCH - LATER - DAY

The burned remains of church. All that
remains is charred rubble and the
collapsed remains of the church bell
tower. A tall wooden burned cross on a
rock rumble foundation still stands
resolute in defiance to what the
building has suffered.

James rides up to the church through
the apple trees towards the ruin.

                    JAMES
          Whoa.

He gets off the horse and walks him the
rest of the way to the pile of ashes.

He stands before the blackened pile of
burned timbers. And the remains of a
collapsed steeple with the chard cross
rising defiantly above the rubble.

He drops the reins and stumbles to the
edge of the ruin. He looks at the
remains of the church. His brother's
church. Unbelieving. He kicks at the
ashes and shakes his head in disbelief.

He hears a woman crying.

James draws his gun and approaches
where the sound is coming from.

On the other side of a tree MELISSA
GREEN COLLINS, late twenties, plain and
simple, wears a gold band on her left
hand. She sits on a stump, head slumped
over. She is sobbing. She is unaware of
James arrival.

His horse lets out a bit of noise and
she looks up, startled.

James points his gun in Melissa's
direction

                    JAMES
          Don't be afraid.

Melissa eyes the gun.

                    MELISSA
          Who are you?

James looks down at the gun in his hand
and lowers it.

James tips his hat.

                    JAMES
          Sorry.
            (pause)
          I'm James. This was my
          brother's church. I came
          to find my him.

She stands up and holds her hand out.

                    MELISSA
          I'm Melissa.

They shake hands.

                    MELISSA (CONT'D)
          Let me take you to him.

She tears up again, wipes her face with
her hankie.

She turns and looks away from the ruin
and towards a small cross planted in
the ground not too far away.

                    MELISSA (CONT'D)
          We buried him over
          there. It was just too
          terrib...

She breaks out in tears again.

James walks over the cross hammered
into the ground. He bends and touches
it and closes his eyes. Then collapses
to his knees.

                    JAMES
               (softly)
          I came as soon as I got
          the letter.
               (pause)
          You sent it six months
          ago but I just got... I
          was in Nevada.Why didn't
          you tell me you were in
          danger?

James pulls a letter from his shirt
pocket, he sits on the ground holding
the letter in one hand and covering his
eyes with the other.

Melissa steps over and gently lifts the
paper from just hand.

                    MELISSA
               (reading)
          Brother. The last time
          we spoke you were
          heading off to war and I
          was going to do Gods
          work. You called me a
          coward for not standing
          up for my beliefs as you
          were doing. I am sorry,
                         (MORE)

                    MELISSA (CONT'D)
but the Lord's way is
not of violence. I could
not follow in your path
though I prayed for the
outcome to be
successful.And I prayed
that you would be safe.
    (pause)
You are a man of action
and I of introspection.
    (pause)
Now I see that action is
sometimes required to
right terrible wrongs. I
have tried to be strong
like you and stand up to
the wrong doers, but
they do not listen.
    (pause)
I need your help. This
is your area, you being
a law man and I but a
humble minister.
    (pause)
Please come to Fort
Howard and help me stop
the evil from ruining
the lives of the good
people here. I have no
more options.
    (pause)
Thank you my brother. I
love you. Tom

Melissa lowers the letter to her side
and looks at James.

                    MELISSA (CONT'D)
          So, you're a lawman?

James nods his head.

                    JAMES
          US Marshal.

He stands and composes himself.

                    JAMES (CONT'D)
          Do you know how my
          brother died?

                    MELISSA
          I think so. Just like
          his letter said, there's
          some bad things going on
          in this town and no one
          can or will stop it.
          Tom... he tried, he was
          slowly getting the
          congregation on his side
          to stand up for what's
          right. Then... Then this
          happened.

                    JAMES
          When?

                    MELISSA
          The night after his last
          sermon...

FLASHBACK BEGINS

INT. CHURCH SUNDAY - MORNING

Thomas McCord is standing at a pulpit
in front of a small church. He is in
the middle of delivering a sermon. All
the farmers and towns people are there
including Ginny, Melissa, Stratton, and
Elizabeth.

                    THOMAS
          If the righteous and the
          meek are to inherit the
          earth then it is time
          for the righteous to do
          more than pray!
            (pause)
          We must not look the
          other way? What if when
          Jesus stumbled as he was
          carrying the cross the
          carpenter looked the
          other way instead of
          lending a helping hand?

The crowd shifts in their pews.

                    THOMAS (CONT'D)
          What if Jesus looked the
          other way when Lazarus
          died? Or when the woman
          was being stoned? What
          if he looked away when
          he saw the money
                         (MORE)

> THOMAS (CONT'D
> changers in the temple
> (pause)
> I am one man. But I do
> not look away. I see who
> the thieves are and I
> call them out!

Thomas points to the back of the
church. Reb and Whitey stand at the
back door.

Reb looks back before he leaves with a
menacing look and points his finger at
Thomas like it was a gun and takes aim
and silently fires. He exits.

> THOMAS (CONT'D)
> There, my brothers and
> sisters, there go the
> servants of Satan. Stand
> with me and we can rid
> the town of their
> evil...

FLASHBACK ENDS

EXT. BURNED CHURCH - DAY

Back to the present.

> MELISSA
> ...and he died that
> night.

                    JAMES
          I think I may have met
          Reb in the saloon.

                    MELISSA
          That's one of his
          places. That and the
          Mayor's house or he's
          with that prostitute,
          Ginny.

James touches the cross on Thomas's
grave.

                    JAMES
          I'm going to find who
          did this to you brother.
          I swear.

                    MELISSA
          Um, you got a place to
          stay?

                    JAMES
          Just thought I'd camp
          out, been doing it a lot
          lately.

                    MELISSA
          Well, we have a second
          cabin on the property,
          you can stay there.

                    JAMES
          Will that be okay with
          your husband?

                    MELISSA
          It's my parents place.

She looks away.

                    MELISSA (CONT'D)
          Henry was killed at
          Antietam.

                    JAMES
          I'm sorry to hear that.
          Do you have any
          children?

                    MELISSA
          We lost Henry junior to
          diphtheria. Now, I'm
          living with my parents.
          I'm sure my father would
          like to meet you. And my
          mother, well if I
          told her that Tom's
          brother was in town and
          I didn't invite you to
          dinner, well, I might be
          disowned.

James smiles.

                    JAMES
          I guess I'm coming to
          dinner at your place.

                    MELISSA
          Wonderful! It's not far,
          just West of the orchard
          over there.

James looks around.

                    JAMES
          Where's your mount?

                    MELISSA
          I walked.

James climbs onto his horse and reaches
down to her climb up.

Melissa takes his hand and swings up to
the back of his horse.

                    JAMES
          Which way did you say
          we're going?

INT. GREEN'S CABIN - EVENING

Interior of a modest and small
homesteader's cabin. James, Melissa sit
at dinner table with her mother
ELIZABETH GREEN and her father STRATTON
GREEN, beard, glasses, heavy set. They
have just finished eating.

Elizabeth and Melissa get up to clear
the dishes. James and Stratton remain
seated continuing the conversation.

                    JAMES
          I wouldn't say that Tom
          and I were close. Oh, we
          loved each other, as
          brothers do, but our
                         (MORE)

                    JAMES (CONT'D)
          natures were so
          different.

                    STRATTON
          My brother and I have
          the same relationship.
          We look at the world
          through different
          lenses. I see it as blue
          and he sees it as red.

                    JAMES
          Tom always liked to use
          his brain.Think things
          through.I'm more of a
          take action type of man.

                    ELIZABETH
          Well, we all appreciated
          how he could explain the
          scripture to us.
          Sometimes the word
          needs a bit of
          explaining so us simple
          minded folk can
          understand what it all
          means.

                    MELISSA
          Now mother, you are not
          simple minded. And if
          there were anyone that
          didn't need the bible
          explained to her it is
          you.

                    STRATTON
               (explaining to James)
          Lizzie used to give the
          bible lessons to the
          children before Thomas
          arrived. I swear she
          recites chapter and
          verse in her sleep
               (Laughs)

Elizabeth slaps him with her dish
towel.

                    ELIZABETH
               (laughing)
          Oh, you stop that!

                    JAMES
               (smiling)
          So, when something would
          happen I used my hands
          to solve the problem,
          but he would stop and
          think about it. You
          might say that he would
          pray over it and then
          take the appropriate
          action.
               (pause)
          Until just now it never
          occurred to me that
          that was what he was
          doing. Praying for
          guidance.
                              (MORE)

                    JAMES (CONT'D)
          Anyway, it's now obvious
          that he spent a good
          deal of time praying
          when he chose to become
          a minister and went off
          to Harvard divinity
          school.

                    ELIZABETH
          Your brother was a good
          man...

                    STRATTON
          The best. The moment
          he came to our community
          you could tell he had a
          character that most
          don't, like he had a
          direct connection with
          the Lord. You could feel
          it.

                    MELISSA
          We had a picnic right
          out in front of the
          cabin just a couple of
          weeks before he was
          killed. The
          congregation want to
          tell him how much we
          appreciated him...

FLASHBACK STARTS

EXT. GREEN'S CABIN - DAY

It is the same beautiful day. Outside
of the house two picnic tables are set
up adorned with a boatload of food.
Kids run around, women are fussing over
food, the men sit around, content.

The CAMERA FOCUSES on the men when
Elizabeth Green comes up to the table
to clear some things off. Thomas sits
in the group of men, still in his
outfit.

                THOMAS
          Mrs. Green, you are
          still the best hostess
          Fort Howard has ever
          seen. I'd stay here just
          for your hospitality.
          Thank you, that was
          delicious.

                ELIZABETH
           (a bit shyly)
          Oh, why thank you
          Thomas.

Elizabeth clears the table more with
Melissa right behind her. Melissa and
Thomas exchange a smile. Stratton sits
next to Thomas and puts his hand the
shoulder of Thomas.

                    STRATTON
          ...Thomas, you've been
          here for what, a year
          now?
             (beat)
          You're the best preacher
          we've had, and we'd like
          to keep it that way
             (beat)
          Going up against the
          Mayor Is… Well, we've
          seen many do it and
          fail. You preach on
          livin' good, doin'
          right, but today... it
          seems you've taken on
          some different
          convictions.

The other men murmur in agreement.
Thomas shifts in his seat, smiling. The
women are at work, but are paying
attention to his response.

                    THOMAS
          Stratton, you've been a
          good friend to me. All
          of you have been good
          friends, welcomed me in
          when I came here, took
          me in.
             (beat)
          But I've also been
          watching how things work
          in this town. There's
                              (MORE)

                    THOMAS (CONT'D)
          only a few of you that
          aren't taking bribes or
          are part of the gang.
             (beat)
          The town lives in terror
          most of the time. I know
          I'm not at my pulpit,
          but the Lord has been
          directing me to the Old
          Testament more and more
          recently. I've seen it
          with an entirely new
          perspective since
          moving here. It's filled
          with corrupt rulers and
          the Lord abhors it...He
          hates it.

A couple of the Farmer's give him a
questioningly look.

                    THOMAS (CONT'D)
          You wanna' call me a
          modern day prophet,
          that's fine. But I'm
          coming in the name of
          God and that's something
          more powerful than they
          will ever know!

The group of men clap for Thomas,
except for Stratton who only smiles.

                    STRATTON
          Here, here.
            (intently at Thomas)
          All I'm saying Thomas,
          is that we like you and
          we wouldn't want
          anything to happen.

One of the other men pipes up, farmer,
WILLIAM REY.

                    WILLIAM
          Thomas, he's right. The
          last preacher was run
          out of town for a
          gambling problem and the
          one before that, some
          say was killed because
          he was being paid off by
          the Mayor and he double
          crossed them.

Thomas smiles and pats William.

                    THOMAS
          It's okay gentlemen. My
          gambling problem is
          under control and money
          doesn't mean much to me
          anymore.

The men show signs of shock and dismay.
Thomas winks and flashes a broad grin.
The men relax when they discover that
Thomas was kidding them.

                         THOMAS (CONT'D)
                    Understand, the reason
                    God had such harsh
                    judgements is that he
                    wanted to turn his
                    people around, to him.
                    Mayor Pierce is a
                    sinner... but a man in
                    need of salvation too.
                    How is someone supposed
                    to repent when no-one is
                    speaking up for what is
                    right? How are they
                    going to know to turn
                    from their evil ways
                         (beat)
                    The word says, "I would
                    welcome any one of them
                    to knock on my door."

The men look frustrated, Thomas picks
up on this.

                         THOMAS (CONT'D)
                    William, from what I
                    hear you used to run
                    with the Mayor's gang,
                    you were a thug.And
                    now look at you.

                    And Clarence, you used
                    to be the town drunk.
                    God got a hold of you
                    and has made you into a
                    model citizen.   (MORE)

                    THOMAS (CONT'D)
          No, I think I'll stay
          God's appointed servant
          here, passionate and
          compassionate.

The men glance at each other, roll
their eyes.

                    THOMAS (CONT'D)
          What?
             (a sly smile)
          Okay, I'll watch myself.
          But I'm not carrying a
          gun and I'm not going to
          shelter myself.
          Understand?

The men lighten up.

                    THOMAS (CONT'D)
          Besides, I've got you
          guys to watch my front
          side, and God to watch
          my backside and I am
          such a bad shot.

A couple of the men laugh slightly.

                    STRATTON
          All right then. Now how
          about some of my wife's
          apple pie?

                    THOMAS
          There's nothing I'd want
          more in the entire
          world.

Elizabeth is just coming to the table
with the pie. All the men smile big as
they lick their chops.

END FLASHBACK

INT. GREEN'S CABIN - EVENING

                    JAMES
               (getting serious)
          How did my brother die?

                    MELISSA
          Like I told you, we
          found him in the
          smoldering church the
          next day after the
          embers cooled down.

                    JAMES
          Listen, I understand
          that you found his
          burned body, but how did
          he come to die in the
          church fire?

                    MELISSA
          The talk around the town
          says that he got drunk
          that night and came back
          to the church, he had a
                              (MORE)

> MELISSA (CONT'D)
> room in the back, and
> must have fallen
> knocking over a lamp.
> The old wood went up
> pretty fast...

> JAMES
> I know Tom, he was no
> teetotaler, but I never
> knew him to have more
> than a couple. Certainly
> not so much as to
> stumble into a lamp ....

> STRATTON
> Sure he liked a nip or
> two, he was human, which
> was one of the things
> that made him likable,
> but he never drank
> to excess, just enough
> to be conversational.

> ELIZABETH
> I've seen Tom and my
> husband a few times on
> the porch enjoying an
> apple jack or two after
> supper. They always had
> a lively conversation...

Stratton smiles and nods.

                    ELIZABETH (CONT'D)
          ...and laughed a lot but
          Tom would always say
          good night after a
          couple. No matter how
          hard he begged him
          to stay for another.

                    STRATTON
          Begged? I never...

Elizabeth gives him a warm hug and they
both smile at the friendly banter.

                    STRATTON (CON'T)
          Yeah, Tom was a good man
          that way, never judged
          another man and wasn't
          afraid to acknowledge
          his own humanity.

                    MELISSA
          Tom never preached fire
          and brimstone. He always
          spoke of God's love for
          us and he lived that
          message.
             (pause)
          This town has a fair mix
          of Yankee and
          Confederate
          homesteaders, there's a
          fair amount of tension
          between the two but
                              (MORE)

MELISSA (CONT'D)
the war ended at the
door of the church. To
Tom we were all equal.

JAMES
You've told me that Tom
thought Mayor Pierce was
behind the bad goings on
around here. Could he
have had something to do
with his death?

MELISSA
Maybe, Tom thought that
the Mayor was up to
something.

JAMES
Like what?

MELISSA
Before the war, the
Ricard Pierce was just
another down on his luck
trapper. The beaver were
pretty much trapped out
and he had never saved
any money.

STRATTON
When the war broke out a
lot of the men headed
East. He stayed behind.
Somehow he weaseled his
(MORE)

                    STRATTON (CONT'D
way into a position of
respectability then got
himself elected Mayor
   (beat)
No one much cared this
is not a very big town
and if someone wanted
the trouble the position
was theirs. When the
war ended there was an
influx of people
escaping the
destruction.
   (beat)
Among the new settlers
was a group of soldiers.
Reb and his bunch. They
didn't come to farm,
they might have moved on
if it weren't for the
Mayor. And that's when
things started to go
bad.

                    MELISSA
Your brother watched as
people lost their
savings to bank
robberies. And their
stock to rustlers.
Bandits would accost
farmers coming back from
the sale of their crops.

                    STRATTON
          Come on out on the porch
          with me James I think I
          have something that can
          take the bite out of
          what you just heard.

                    ELIZABETH
          Now Stratton...

                    STRATTON
          Now you stop with the
          comments. This man has
          been through a lot and a
          bit of night air will be
          good for him.

                    ELIZABETH
          Night air? So that's
          what you're calling it
          now.

Stratton waves a dismissive hand
towards his wife and ushers James out
the door.

                    STRATTON
          Marriage isn't for the
          weak hearted...

As the door closes...

                    ELIZABETH
          For both parties...

EXT. GREEN'S CABIN - NIGHT

A lovely night on the porch in front of
Green's cabin. No light except for that
of the moon. Crickets chirping etc.

James and Stratton sit in a couple of
chairs and look out into the night.

Stratton opens a wooden box that sits
next to his chair. In it is a bottle of
whiskey and a couple of cups. He offers
James a drink.

                    STRATTON
          I find that a wee taste
          after dinner is good for
          the digestion.

James takes the cup.

                    JAMES
          Thanks, that's what I
          always say too.

The two smile at the joke.

Stratton pulls out a pipe and stuffs it
with tobacco and lights it. He draws on
the pipe a few good times to get it
going then leans back in his chair.
They sit a bit without any words
enjoying the quiet moment.

                    STRATTON
          I said it inside but it
          bares repeating, your
          brother was good man.
          Anyone would have been
          proud to call him son or
          brother.

He holds up his cup in a toast to Tom.
James clinks cups.

                    STRATTON (CONT'D)
          I'm sorry for your loss.

                    JAMES
             (in slightly bitter
          voice)
          Yeah.
             (beat)
          A loss that shouldn't
          have
          happened.

He sips.

                    STRATTON
          So, what do you figure
          on doing now?

James fingers the letter from Thomas.

                    JAMES
          I know my brother. He
          was a man of God for
          certain but not one
          of those "hell and
                              (MORE)

                    JAMES (CONT'D)
          damnation" types
          either.Like you said, he
          liked to have a nip or
          two but he would never
          drink to the point where
          he would, could do
          anything to cause harm
          or damage.
            (beat)
          No, something happened
          to him and I'm not
          leaving until I find out
          what.

Melissa exits the house. She is holding
Thomas's tin box, she hands it to
James.

                    MELISSA
          This was your brothers.

James accepts the box and looks at it
in his hands.

                    MELISSA (CONT'D)
          After the fire, I found
          this in what was left of
          the church office.

James is afraid to open it.

                    JAMES
          What's inside?

                    MELISSA
          I don't know. Wasn't my
          place to snoop.

James opens the lid. Stratton lights up
a lantern and holds it allowing the
interior to be illuminated.

James sets the box on the top of the
wooden box and removes the contents. He
pulls out some papers that appear to be
legal type documents, birth certificate
etc. And sets them down.

He holds a stiff card that's a blurred
photo of two boys.

                    JAMES
          I remember the day this
          was taken. Imagine two
          little boys holding
          still for that long. It
          frustrated the heck out
          of the photographer. He
          took several poses and
          in the end this was the
          one least blurry.
             (smiles)
          Our father was so damned
          mad. Each pose cost him
          out of his pocket.

James stares at the image. Then sets it
down. He fishes back into the box and
pulls out a locket. Another bitter/

sweet smile and he opens it. A picture
of a woman is inside.

                    JAMES (CONT'D)
          This is our mother.
            (beat)
          She always told me that
          I needed to watch out
          for my younger brother.
          I promised that I
          would...

James lowers his head. Melissa places
her hand on his shoulder. James sniffs
back the beginning of tears and looks
back up.

He closes the locket and lovingly
places it on top of the photo. He
reaches back into the box and pulls out
a gold ring.

                    JAMES (CONT'D)
          And this was her wedding
          band. Mother didn't want
          it buried with her, she
          wanted one of us to use
          it when the time came.

James holds the ring up to Melissa who
suddenly becomes embarrassed. James
notices but makes no comment. James
pulls out a few more items but quickly
sets them aside.

At the bottom of the box James removes
a leather bound journal book. It is
tied with a black ribbon. He looks
expectantly to Stratton and Melissa.

James unties the ribbon and opens the
book.

                    JAMES (CONT'D)
          This looks like Tom's
          hand writing.

He turns a few pages.

                    JAMES (CONT'D)
          This is his journal. Did
          you know he kept this?

                    STRATTON
          Well, this is new to me,
          but then not many admit
          that they keep a diary.

                    MELISSA
             (slightly agitated)
          No!
             (beat)
          Uh, why would I have
          know?

                    JAMES
          I meant nothing by the
          question. I'm surprised
          that he kept a record of
          his thoughts, maybe I
          can find some hint of
                              (MORE)

                    JAMES (CONT'D)
          who might have wanted to
          have him harmed.

                    MELISSA
          Oh, yes. So, its getting
          late I think I'll be
          calling it an evening.
          Good night father.

Melissa kisses his cheek.

                    MELISSA (CONT'D)
          And good night James.

She enters the cabin.

                    JAMES
          What do you think got
          into her?

                    STRATTON
          Well, you might be
          careful with the
          information that you get
          when you read that
          thing.

James hold the book and looks at it.

                    STRATTON (CONT'D)
          It may not just contain
          information concerning
          who may have hated
          Thomas. If you get my
          meaning…

                    JAMES
               (puzzled)
          Uh, yeah, I guess so.

INT. GREEN'S CABIN - BEDROOM - LATER -
NIGHT

James lights a lantern and sits on the
edge of a cot. He holds Thomas's diary
in his hands. He takes a deep breath
and slowly opens it.

                    JAMES
          Now, let's see if you
          have anything to tell me
          little brother.

James gets comfortable and starts
reading.

                    THOMAS (V.O.)
          The West. A land full of
          promise for many. For
          me, it is the land of my
          destiny. Though I left a
          comfortable life,God's
          calling to preach his
          Gospel is an exciting
          task - and I cannot wait
          to get started.

James looks up and stares to the wall
-- thinking. He turns back to reading.
A montage follows of him reading
through the first half of the diary.

                    THOMAS (V.O)
          (CONT'D)
          Corruption! It seethes
          from within our
          community. Our own
          leaders are testaments
          to it. As Galatians 6:8
          tells us, For he that
          soweth to his flesh
          shall of the flesh reap
          corruption; but he that
          soweth to the Spirit
          shall of the Spirit reap
          life everlasting.

                    James turns a page
          and continues reading

                    THOMAS (V.O.)
          (CONT'D)
          I am convinced that the
          Mayor has his hands in
          the cookie jar. This
          community has been
          without any form of law
          for many years and
          this one man has come
          into control of more
          than just the town
          council.

James turns a couple of pages more.

                    THOMAS (V.O.)
(CONT'D)
It is unbelievable how
brazen the Mayor is in
his offer that I should
be a part of his
"venture". He actually
offered me money if I
were to look away and
keep my congregation
from snooping around his
affairs. This is not the
type of ministry I
thought I would find
when I came West. But I
intend to do more than
sit back quietly and
watch these good people
be corrupted.

James turns a few more pages than he
stops and sits up taking notice.

                    THOMAS (V.O.)
(CONT'D)
I was attacked today.
Reb, that man who works
for the Mayor, He
actually came into the
church and physically
accosted me! He told me
to get into line, that a
little push and a shove
is nothing compared to
what I could expect if I
                    (MORE)

                    THOMAS (V.O.)
          (CONT'D)… didn't start
          cooperating.
             (beat)
          Melissa Green came by
          just after this
          incident. She asked me
          if I was okay and it was
          only then that I
          realized that I had
          blood on my forehead
             (beat)
          Such a lovely
          girl.Perhaps I shall
          inquire with her father
          if I could court her...

James looks up from his reading and
nods now understanding Stratton's
words.

                    THOMAS (V.O.)
          (CONT'D)
          Today I followed the
          Mayor and Reb to an
          abandoned trapper's
          fort. They carried with
          them bulging saddle bags
          and when they left the
          bags were empty. I snuck
          inside. The rooms were
          filled with all types of
          stolen goods and crates
          of weapons.
                    (MORE)

                    THOMAS (V.O.)
          (CONT'D)
          I drew a map to the
          location. I hear that
          the army will soon be
          here to assume a
          protective presence for
          the settlers. Being
          representatives of the
          federal government I
          plan on presenting the
          map in the hopes that
          they will uphold the
          laws of this country.

James turns another page and a folded
piece of paper drops to the floor. He
picks it up and opens it. It is
Thomas's map.

EXT. BLACKSMITH SHOP - DAY

James rides through town. He stops and
asks a man a question. Thanks him and
rides in the direction the man pointed
in.

James brings horse to a stop in front
of the blacksmith's. He dismounts and
makes a quick check of his horse's
hooves and shakes his head finding
something to be concerned about.

Loud voices come out of the interior of
the shop.

James lowers the horses leg and moves
to the door. The voices get louder the
closer he gets.

INT. BLACKSMITH SHOP - CONTINUOUS - DAY

James enters the shop cautiously.

He finds Buford and Whitey giving the
Solomon a hard time, holding his hand
to the fire, one is pumping the bellows
and getting the coals nice and hot.

                    BUFORD
          So, again, when you
          goin' to make the rent
          payment this month?

                    SOLOMON
          I already told you,
          things have been slow.
          The army tells me that
          they want me to look at
          their horses next week
          and maybe fix a couple
          things too.

                    BUFORD
          That don't solve the
          problem we have right
          now

Buford pushes the Solomon's hand closer
to the heat.

Solomon struggles and groans from the
burning pain.

James steps further into the shop with
his gun drawn.

                JAMES
          Just what are you boys
          doin'?

                WHITEY
          Business. Between the
          three of us and it's
          none of yours.

James cocks his pistol.

                JAMES
          Makin' it mine right
          now.Let him go and get
          out of here.

                BUFORD
          We know who you are, the
          dead preacher's brother.
          Wasn't afraid of him and
          not afraid of you.

James hits Buford's wrist holding
Blacksmith with butt of gun handle.

Buford lets out a shriek and let's go.
He rubs his wrist.

                BUFORD
          You could of broken it!

                    JAMES
          You could of burned his
          hand making it
          impossible for him to
          earn the rent you boys
          seem to desperately
          want.
               (to Blacksmith)
          You going to pay these
          business men what they
          want next week?

                    SOLOMON
          I swear.

                    JAMES
          Then there you have it.
          Next week. And ask
          nicely next time.

James points gun at thugs at Buford and
Whitey.

                    JAMES (CONT'D)
          Now beat it.

Buford and Whitey exit.

                    JAMES (CONT'D)
          Can you look at my
          horse? I think his front
          right shoe needs tending
          to.

                    SOLOMON
          Thanks…
            (beat)
          You're the preacher's
          brother. Heard you had
          come into town... Sorry
          about the Reverend, your
          brother. He was a good
          man, the best.

                    JAMES
          So I gather.
            (beat)
          So how about my horse?

They exit.

INT. SALOON - DAY

The next day, James walks into the
saloon. Place is half full. Mostly
Settlers, a few Soldiers and Reb with
Buford, Whitey, Slim, Lefty, and Ginny.
James steps up to the bar and orders a
drink which he takes and turns to
survey the room.

The soldiers pay him no attention. The
settlers act nervous when they see that
Reb is giving him the evil eye.

James's eyes fall on a table occupied
by a lone soldier. He finishes his
drink and orders another and one for
the soldier. He carries them over to
the soldiers table.

                    JAMES
          Mind if I join you?

He sets the one drink in front of
CAPTAIN LEWIS.

Lewis looks up to James, smiles and
accepts the drink and motions to an
empty chair.

                    CAPTAIN LEWIS
          Thanks.

                    JAMES
          Wanted to introduce
          myself to...

                    CAPTAIN LEWIS
          No need for that
          Marshal. You've kind of
          made an impression
          around here.

James looks around the room. Now all
eyes are on him and the captain.

                    JAMES
          Guess I'm not surprised.
          Listen Captain, I might
          need your help.

                    CAPTAIN LEWIS
          Not sure how that can
          happen, we're forbidden
          by law to participate in
          domestic issues. Our
                              (MORE)

                    CAPTAIN LEWIS
                    (CONST'D)
          ...mission is keeping
          settlers safe, yours is
          keeping the peace.

                    JAMES
          Well, things aren't
          always as cut and dried
          as that, you see any
          fighting during the
          war?

Lewis studies his glass.

                    CAPTAIN LEWIS
          Gettysburg. 20th Maine.

                    JAMES
          Your unit held Little
          Round Top.
               (beat)
          War might have been lost
          if you boys didn't hold
          the confederates like
          you did.

                    CAPTAIN LEWIS
          Sometimes I wonder
          though. Lost my brother
          there at the High Water
          Mark.

                    JAMES
          A lot of Americans died
          in those three days...
          North and South. Many
          not really knowing or
          understanding what they
          were fighting for.
             (beat)
          On one level it was
          pretty cut and dried.
          But on another level
          they were just a bunch
          of kids killing each
          other. Americans.

                    CAPTAIN LEWI
          Sounds like you may have
          gotten a snoot full
          yourself.

                    JAMES
          12th Mass. Saw my fair
          share.

                    CAPTAIN LEWIS
          Seems to me I heard you
          boys were at Gettysburg
          too...

                    JAMES
          And second Bull Run...
          Antietam...
          Fredericksburg...

Captain raises his glass stopping the
conversation from spiraling down into
depression.

                    CAPTAIN LEWIS
               Here's to them all.

James raises his glass and they down
their drinks.

                    CAPTAIN LEWIS
               (CONT'D)
               Okay, so what're you
               asking?

                    JAMES
               If I need support...
               IF... I want to know I
               can come to you.

                    CAPTAIN LEWIS
               You do understand that I
               have only a small
               compliment of men
               stationed here with me.
               We were sent out here to
               prepare for a larger
               force to arrive later
               next year.

                    JAMES
               Don't worry, I can
               usually handle things
               myself but sometimes...

Captain Lewis nods to Reb and his men.

                    CAPTAIN LEWIS
          Obviously something to
          do with Reb over there
          and his holdouts from …
          the Confederate army.
          Story is that he road
          with Quantrill for a bit
          before coming out West.

James pours them another round.

                    JAMES
          Very perceptive captain.

Captain Lewis smiles.

                    CAPTAIN LEWIS
          So what's going on? Got
          something to do with
          your brother?

                    JAMES
          I don't have anything
          solid right now but,
          yeah, my brother was
          trying to stand up to
          the Mayor.

                    CAPTAIN LEWIS
          Well, the Mayor, I may
          not be able to help with
          but seeing as how this
          involves "enemies of the
          state". Quantrill's
          Raiders and all,I think
                              (MORE)

                    CAPTAIN LEWIS
               (CONT'D)
          I might be able to offer
          help.BUT, at least tell
          me when you find what
          you're looking for,
          BEFORE, you need me and
          my men to get caught up
          in the local issues?

                    JAMES
               (smiles)
          Of course.

INT. TOWN STORE - DAY

James enters trader's store looking for
stuff. At the counter stand the same
thugs who were at the blacksmith shop
earlier. They are talking to MRS.
TRUMBLE the proprietor.

                    BUFORD
          Now you know that we let
          you slide on your rent
          last month. Right?

                    MRS. TRUMBLE
               (nervously)
          Y-yes.

                    BUFORD
          And you know how the
          rent has to be paid on
          time. Right?

Mrs. Trumble nods in acknowledgement)

Whitey starts to poke around the trade goods in the store. Messing things up. Acting like a bull in a china shop. He knocks a porcelain vase over and it smashes on the floor.

                    WHITEY
          Oops!

Mrs. Trumble looks at the mess. She says nothing but looks up and sees James in the open door. Her eyes flash wide asking for help.

                    BUFORD
          It's interesting how
          much hard earned money
          can be lost just trying
          to replace accidentally
          broken inventory.

Whitey lifts up another item, ready to drop it too.

James pulls his gun and cocks the hammer. Whitey and Buford turn at the sound.

                    BUFORD (CONT'D)
          Is there some sort of
          alarm bell that
          calls you to get in the
          way of us doing our
          jobs?

                    JAMES
          Why don't you set that
          down, gently and back
          away from the counter.

Buford nods to Whitey, who sets item
down and they take a step back from the
counter.

                    BUFORD
          You know that she owes
          rent. We let her slide
          last month but... we
          gotta makea living too.
          Right?

                    MRS. TRUMBLE
          It's true Marshal, but
          business has been slow.
          Not just for me but the
          whole town. Ever since
          the end of the war money
          has been tight and folks
          are hanging on to what
          they got.

Buford cleans his nails.

                    BUFORD
          Heard that too.

                    JAMES
          Well, threats won't get
          you paid.

                    WHITEY
          It was an accident.

                    JAMES
          Accidents won't either

                    MRS. TRUMBLE
          The army has made
          arrangements to order
          supplies through my
          store. Next month I'll
          have more than enough to
          pay for all three
          months. Can't you wait?

               James still
          holding his gun.

                    JAMES
          Yeah.

Buford eyes the gun.

                    BUFORD
          Sure, I think we can
          manage that.

Buford gives Whitey a nod and they turn
to leave. He stops at door and
addresses Mrs. Trumble

                    BUFORD (CONT'D)
          You know that the
          marshal won't be around
          forever to help you
          manage your business
                         (MORE)

                    BUFORD (CONT'D)
          affairs. I suggest you
          get a bit smarter...

Buford and Whitey exit.

                    MRS. TRUMBLE
          Thank God you came. It's
          a blessing to have you
          here. It's like you were
          sent to help us.

                    JAMES
          I'm not so sure about
          that.
              (beat)
          But I agree that maybe
          you should mind your
          books a bit closer so
          you don't need anyone's
          help in the future.

                    MRS. TRUMBLE
          Since Harold went off to
          the war I've been
          struggling. Lost him at
          Shiloh.

                    JAMES
          I'm sorry.

EXT. MAYOR'S HOUSE - PORCH - DAY

The Mayor sits at small table sipping
coffee, Reb stands nearby.

Buford Buford and Whitey stand in front
of Mayor hats in hand

                    BUFORD
          That reverends brother
          is a problem!

                    MAYOR
          Which means what?

                    WHITEY
          He kept us from
          collecting the rent at
          the blacksmith's like
          you told us to do.

                    BUFORD
          And the general store.

                    MAYOR
          Were you doing anything
          that might cause someone
          to pull a gun?

                    BUFORD
          Nothing that we ain't t
          done before.

                    WHITEY
          Yeah we were just
          encouraging some
          cooperation

                    BUFORD
          Yeah, like giving them a
          good reason to pay now
          instead of wait.

                    MAYOR
You were going to hurt
him?

                    BUFORD
Not much just enough to
make a point.

                    WHITEY
And get him to pay.

                    MAYOR
And...?

                    BUFORD
He'll pay next week
after his work for the
blue bellies is
finished.

                    MAYOR
I can't approve of this
McCord getting in the
way of my business.

                    MAYOR (CONT'D)
But it looks like he
might have helped me you
idiots! You were going
to burn the man...

                    WHITEY
Yep we were...

                    MAYOR
          And make it so he
          couldn't earn a living
          and so he couldn't pay
          me rent!

                    BUFORD
          Ah...

                    MAYOR
          I don't want to own the
          blacksmith company! I
          just want him to pay me
          rent and keep paying for
          as long as he can. Get
          it?

                    WHITEY
          So we can't hurt people?

                    MAYOR
          No, I didn't say that,
          but you have to do it my
          when in the manner that
          I tell you. Collecting
          rent is just that
          nothing more.

Buford and Whitey shift on their feet.

                    MAYOR (CONT'D)
          Now, if you return with
          no rent, then I may have
          another task for you
          that might put the fear
                              (MORE)

                    MAYOR (CONT'D)
          of God into him or
          anyone else who holds
          back on me. Now get out
          of my sight before I ask
          Reb to demonstrate what
          I mean on the two of
          you.

Buford and Whitey exit.

                    MAYOR
             (to Reb)
          It looks like we may
          have a problem.

                    REB
          Yes it does, what do you
          want me to do?

                    MAYOR
          Nothing, not yet, I need
          to see what he is up to.
          Watch him.

                    REB
          You got it.

Reb exits.

Mayor sips his coffee lost in thought.

EXT. GREEN FARM - MORNING

Melissa is feeding the chickens in the
yard under a large tree.

James steps out onto the porch of the
cabin with a cup of coffee in his hand.

James enjoys the moment watching
Melissa scattering the feed amongst the
birds. There is a grace to her
movements and James enjoys the moment.

Melissa doesn't notice that she is
being watched.

She finishes but is pestered by one of
the chickens.

                    MELISSA
               (to the chickens)
          I've fed you all. Don't
          act like you didn't get
          any. Shoo now!

She turns and heads for the cabin, sees
James watching her.

EXT. GREEN'S CABIN - CONTINUOUS - DAY

                    MELISSA
               (embarrassed)
          Oh! Morning. I didn't
          see you standing there.

She sets the feed pail on the porch and
makes to adjust her hair.

                    JAMES
          You know, the morning
          sun gives your hair a
          glow, kinda like a halo.

                    MELISSA
          Well, I'm no angel or a
          saint for that matter.

                    JAMES
          I was thinking more
          along the lines of a
          work of art.

James gives a big grin.

Melissa is left speechless at the
compliment.

                    JAMES (CONT'D)
          Listen... I wanted to
          let you know that I
          found something in
          Thomas' journal that
          could be what I need to
          prove that the Mayor is
          up to no good and
          possibly even was the
          one who had my brother
          killed.

Melissa sits next to James.

                    MELISSA
          What is it? What did you
          find?

James reaches into his vest and removes
a folded piece of paper. And unfolds
it.

                    JAMES
          This is a map that Tom
          drew showing the
          location of where he
          said the Mayor has
          hidden a stash of stolen
          property.

Melissa looks at the map.

                    MELISSA
          I don't know how to read
          this. I don't recognize
          any of this.

                    JAMES
          When we were kids Tom
          and I would play Indian
          scout. We would make
          maps of the woods and
          fields as though we were
          going to use them to
          help settlers get to
          Oregon.
                (beat)
          We drew our maps using a
          sort of a code so if the
          map were ever to be
          stolen the bad guys
          wouldn't be able to use
          it.

Melissa looks at James with question
marks in her eyes.

                    JAMES
          This is drawn just like
          one of those. Tom used
          our code! See, that's
          our symbol for North...
          and this is a stream...
          a forest... anyway...
            (beat)
          I can use this to find
          the old trapper's fort
          he says houses the
          Mayor's cache.

                    MELISSA
          Are you going to find
          it?

                    JAMES
          Yes, today. I wanted to
          tell you in case...

                    MELISSA
          Are you going alone?

                    JAMES
          Yes. It'll be safer that
          way but should you think
          something has happened
          to me I want you to go
          to Captain Lewis and
          tell him. He might be of
          some help.

James removes another piece of paper
from his vest.

                    JAMES (CONT'D)
          This is a copy of Tom's
          map. I redrew it using
          an actual map of the
          area.

He hands the new map to Melissa.

                    JAMES (CONT'D)
          You should be able to
          find me if you think you
          need to.

She takes the map and looks at it.

                    MELISSA
               (recognition)
          I know where this is.
          But I never saw a
          fort...

                    JAMES
          Maybe it's hidden
          somehow. I don't know
          but Tom wouldn't have
          written it if it wasn't
          there.

EXT. FOREST- DAY

MONTAGE - James follows map to old
trappers fort

James is seen riding North. Ft. Howard
in the distance.

James comes to a pause at the top of an
open field. He checks the map.

James comes to a stream and pauses
allowing his horse to drink. He checks
map and sees a forest in front of him

James rides through thick forest.
Ducking branches.

James comes to a stop. He can see an
overgrown structure but it is well
hidden. He dismounts and walks
cautiously towards it.

END OF MONTAGE

EXT. TRAPPERS FORT - DAY

A small stockade almost completely
overgrown.

James ties his horse to a branch and
draws is gun. He cautiously approaches
an opening in the wall of greenery. And
steps through the gate of the old fort.

I/E. TRAPPERS FORT - DAY

There are two rows of cabins that front
onto a small yard. The over growth of
the exterior has given way to what can
only be described as a storage yard.
Crates and barrels are stacked up next
to the walls of the cabins in a very
haphazard way.

James slowly enters the yard and looks around. He reads labels painted on crates. He pries open a barrel and discovers rifles.

He goes to the cabin doors and opens them one at a time looking into them briefly and moving on. He goes to another door and enters.

INT. TRAPPERS FORT - CABIN - DAY

A dark small space. The beam of light cast into it from the open door illuminates more boxes along with trunks and small casks.

James sees a lantern and strikes a match lighting it. The light from the lantern reveals more, a lot more. There are long boxes the top of one is open revealing inside new rifles. Small kegs of powder line the wall. On a table are several cash boxes. He opens one and sees it filled with gold coins.

He replaces the lantern and blows it out.

EXT. TRAPPERS FORT - DAY

James exits the fort quickly and mounts his horse and heads back towards town.

EXT. GREEN'S CABIN - DAY

James rides up, and dismounts, while
Melissa is shelling peas in a large
bowl on her lap.

                    JAMES
          I found it.

                    MELISSA
          What?

                    JAMES
          The Mayor's cache. It's
          more than booty, weapons
          and TNT.

                    MELISSA
          Oh my goodness.

                    JAMES
          Enough for a small army.

                    MELISSA
          You better tell Captain
          Lewis.

She stands up, places the bowl on her
chair. She hugs James.

He turns and mounts his horse. And
rides away.

```
EXT. ARMY ENCAMPMENT - DAY

James rides into town through the main
gate and heads to the army encampment
at the far end of the town.

He comes to a stop at a tent that is
larger than the others with an awning
rigged in front of it. Some chairs and
a table are set up under the awning.

Captain Lewis is seated at the table
reviewing paperwork.

A soldier grabs the bridle of James'
horse as he dismounts and approaches
the Captain

                CAPTAIN LEWIS
          Ah, Marshal. Welcome to
          camp "pain in my rear".

Lewis stands as he rubs his rear and
points to one of the chairs.

                CAPTAIN LEWIS
          (CONT'D)
          Please have a seat and
          join me in this
          luxurious splendor.

James sits.

                CAPTAIN LEWIS
          (CONT'D)
          What brings you here
          McCord?
```

                    JAMES
          I've got him.

                    CAPTAIN LEWIS
          Got who?

James places the map in front of Lewis
on the table.

                    JAMES
          Pierce!
            (pause)
          My brother followed the
          Mayor to this abandoned
          trapper's stockade. The
          Mayor is using it to
          cache his stolen goods.

                    CAPTAIN LEWIS
          So you've seen the Mayor
          with these stolen goods?

                    JAMES
          Well, no but...

                    CAPTAIN LEWIS
          But, first of all that's
          your area of the law not
          mine. Second... just
          what can you do about it
          if you haven't seen him
          with the stolen items?
          Even if your brother
          drew a map.

                    CAPTAIN LEWIS
          (CONT'D)
          Don't you even know the
          laws that you enforce?

                    JAMES
          But, as I was about to
          say, I just came from
          there using this map,
          and what I saw not only
          included stolen
          property but also a
          large number of rifles
          and powder all crated
          nice and neat, ready for
          shipment.

Lewis sits up and leans closer to
James.

                    CAPTAIN LEWIS
          Describe "large number".

                    JAMES
          To me it looks like he
          could arm a small army
          or a very large gang of
          outlaws.

                    CAPTAIN LEWIS
          Hmmm. So, do you know
          why the army sent us
          here?

                    JAMES
          Yes, to protect the
          influx of settlers. No?

                    CAPTAIN LEWIS
          This territory is not
          fully under the
          jurisdiction of the
          federal government.
          There was concern in
          Washington that there
          might be elements of the
          Confederacy who might
          choose to continue the
          fight out West.

                    JAMES
          That explains all the
          Southern types I've had
          the pleasure of meeting
          recently.

                    CAPTAIN LEWIS
          Reb and his boys for
          instance?

                    JAMES
          Yes and others from my
          brother's congregation.
          But those are good
          people, I don't see any
          danger coming from them.
          But they lost. Why the
          concern?

                    CAPTAIN LEWIS
          The concern is that
          these Confederates are
          diehards. To them the
          war isn't over, will
          never be over. They
          still want to establish
          their own country and
          perpetuate their
          misguided policy of
          using humans as their
          slaves.
             (beat)
          Our real job here is to
          put a lid on it and keep
          another war from
          starting.

                    JAMES
          Well, I can't say that
          there were enough
          weapons and supplies to
          wage a war but there
          certainly is enough
          there to give it a good
          start.

                    CAPTAIN LEWIS
          Well, then, it looks
          like our jobs have
          become entwined. And all
          this revolves around the
          Mayor.

                    JAMES
          Indeed it looks that
          way.

INT. MAYOR'S HOUSE - OFFICE - EVENING

Mayor is sitting at a desk going over
ledger book. Reb enters the Mayor's
parlor and sits down without being
invited and makes himself overly
comfortable.

Not looking up from his work the Mayor
addresses Reb.

                    MAYOR
          I take it that you have
          something to tell me.

                    REB
          Not going to offer me a
          drink?

                    MAYOR
          You know where it is.
          Help yourself.

Reb gets up and walks to decanter and
pours a drink.

                    REB
          Want one?

                    MAYOR
          If I have to put up with
          you, then yeah.

Reb pours a second whiskey then walks
over to the Mayor and sets it in front
of him then sits down.

                    REB
          I watched the preacher's
          brother ride out of town
          today. He headed North.

                    MAYOR

          Follow him?

                    REB
          Nope, so I don't know
          where he went, lots to
          see and do up North...

                    MAYOR
          And find.

                    REB
          It would have been too
          late for me to have
          followed him.

He takes a sip.

                    REB (CONT'D)
          But without knowing
          where to look he
          couldn't have found the
          stockade. Unless someone
          told him. I didn't.
              (beat)
          Did you?

The Mayor gives Reb a stern look and
leans in closer to him.

                    MAYOR
          I think that somebody
          may be forgetting who is
          running this operation.

                    REB
          I haven't forgotten
          anything, like who's
          supplying the muscle for
          instance.

He stares back at the Mayor.

                    REB (CONT'D)
          Have you?

                    MAYOR
          Of course not.
            (beat)
          I think it's time for
          you to have a little
          "chat" with McCord. See
          if he can be
          "persuaded" to leave us
          alone.

Reb smiles as he punches his fist into
the palm of his hand.

                    REB
          And if he doesn't back
          off?

                    MAYOR
If he doesn't respond to
the "nice" way... we
step it up to the next
level.

                    REB
Kill him?

                    MAYOR
We can't go about
killing everyone. We're
going to be the heads of
a new country and we
have to keep our heads
above that sort of
 dirty work.

                    REB
But if...

                    MAYOR
Only as a last resort
   (beat)
Bring him to me in the
back room at the saloon
tomorrow night. We'll
see then.

Reb bows in an affected manor

                    REB
As you say your majesty.

                    MAYOR
               (smiling)
          Mr. President will do
          just fine.

                    REB
          You bet boss.

Reb exits.

EXT. STREET - NIGHT

James exits the saloon and walks to his
horse. As he is about to untie it from
the hitching post Ginny appears from
around the corner of a building and
leans against it looking to James.

                    GINNY
          Hey! McCord.

James looks to her. She signals for him
to come over to her.

                    GINNY (CONT'D)
          I've got some
          information on who
          killed your brother.

                    JAMES
               (interested)
          What do you know?

                    GINNY
          Not here. They might see
          us.

She turns the looks behind herself.

                    GINNY (CONT'D)
          Back here off the
          street.

EXT. BEHIND BUILDING - CONTINUOUS -
NIGHT

Ginny leads James back behind the
building and stops.

                    JAMES
          Okay. Now tell me...

                    GINNY
            (alluringly)
          I will, in a moment.
            (beat)
          Just want to see if
          you're like your
          brother.

Ginny moves in closer to James and
starts to run her fingers through his
hair.

He brushes her hand away.

                    JAMES
            (annoyed)
          This isn't what I came
          for. You said you have
          information concerning
          Tom's death so tell
          me...

Ginny looks past James and sees Reb
with two thugs rounding the corner of
the building.

She smiles, tears the collar down from
her blouse, musses her hair and smears
some dirt on the side of her face.

                    GINNY
               (yells)
          Help!

                    JAMES
          What...

Reb steps up to Ginny and the henchmen
line up on either side of James.

                    REB
          Hey baby doll what's
          going on?

Ginny grabs his arm in a desperate
fashion.

                    GINNY
          He's just like his
          brother Reb. I wasn't
          doing nothing. Then he
          grabs me and...

                    REB
          Just like the preacher
          huh? Well Mr. Yankee
          lawman. We don't cotton
          much to you blue bellies
                         (MORE)

                    REB (CONT'D)
          messing around with our
          women folk.

Reb punches James in the gut. The thugs
grab his arms and stand him up
straight.

                    REB (CONT'D)
          Obviously they don't
          teach manners in them
          fancy Northern schools.

Another punch to the gut then as James
raise his head Reb gives him a right
cut to the face.

                    REB (CONT'D)
          Now, if I didn't want to
          end up like my brother I
          would get on my horse
          and ride out of this
          town while I could.

                    REB (CONT'D)
            (beat)
          If you understand my
          drift.

Another punch to the gut. James
collapses to the ground and the thugs
take their turn kicking at him.

                    REB (CONT'D)
          (to the thugs)
          Come on, let's see if he
          gets the message.

Reb puts his arm around Ginny's
shoulder and start to leave. Ginny
stops at James and bends down to speak.

                    GINNY
          I guess you are like
          your brother. A man of
          no action... too bad.

She runs her finger along the side of
James cheek seductively. Reb yanks her
up.

                    REB
          All right, let's get out
          of here.

They exit.

EXT. BEHIND THE BUILDING - NIGHT

LATER

James lies face down in the dirt. He
opens his eyes slowly. He is in pain.
He tries to move and clutches his
stomach letting out a groan.

Slowly, painfully he drags himself up
onto his feet using crates and barrels
against the wall. He staggers to the
front of the building and stops at the

corner. Several drunks walk past him
and pay no attention.

EXT. STREET - NIGHT

James staggers to his horse and
painfully climbs on it. He turns it and
rides out through the gate.

EXT. GREENS CABIN - NIGHT

James rides up to the Green's cabin. He
is bent over in pain. Stops and
dismounts with difficulty and
approaches the porch. He steps up but
collapses knocking over a chair and
making a loud noise.

Stratton exits the house with his
shotgun ready. Elizabeth and Melissa
are right behind him. They see James,
beat up and in a mess on the porch and
help him inside.

EXT. BURNED OUT CHURCH - MORNING

It's Sunday, the congregation has
assembled at the sight of the burned
church. They stand or sit on a
collection of chairs and benches
brought from home. They face the steps
that lead into the sanctuary.

The Greens arrive in their wagon. They
help James down and together they walk
to the front of the congregation where
they sit.

Everyone is silent. No one really knows
what to do. There is no preacher.
Finally Melissa stands and steps up
onto the front steps.

                    MELISSA
          Good morning.

Nods and random voices of good mornings
in return from the congregation.

                    MELISSA (CONT'D)
               (hesitantly)
          We, uh... We don't have
          a minister here to lead
          us in worship today.
               (beat)
          What we do have is this
          burned church and...

She points into the orchard.

                    MELISSA (CONT'D)
          A grave where our
          minister lies buried,
          Thomas McCord.

All heads drop in prayer and thought.

                    MELISSA (CONT'D)
          The question is; why did
          Reverend McCord die? And
          don't any one of you
          repeat the awful lie
          that it was an accident!
                    (MORE)

                    MELISSA (CONT'D)
Thomas was killed.He was
murdered because he got
in the way of the Mayor.
        (beat)
And none of us, myself
included, had to moral
fortitude to stand with
him. Thomas died because
he was trying to help
us, to do what was best
for us. But we let him
down and in so doing we
let ourselves down too
        (beat)
Now we have another
McCord here with us and
he too is trying to do
the right thing, the
moral thing and take a
stand against evil
        (beat)
The presence of James
McCord has given us a
second chance to do what
the Lord wants us to do.
Not for our own personal
needs but for our entire
community.
        (beat)
The other night James
was beat up by the
Mayor's men. Are we
going to stand by and
                    (MORE)

                    MELISSA (CONT'D)
          let the Mayor intimidate
          us and beat us into
          submission?

Melissa's words have not moved the
congregation. They sit with lips sealed
shut. Afraid to speak.William Rey
standing speaks up.

                    WILLIAM REY
          Are you and your family
          willing to lose all that
          you have worked for to
          go poking around in a
          hornet's nest? Are you
          Stratton? Elizabeth?

Melissa looks to her parents who sit
silent and make no move or response.

                    WILLIAM REY
                    (CONT'D)
          That's what I thought.
          Reverend Thomas was the
          best man we ever had as
          a minister. He did look
          after us but we all know
          what the result was. I'm
          sorry Marshal McCord for
          your loss and for the
          beating you took but we
          don't have a fight in
          us…but this is your job
          not ours.

He sits and his wife gives him a good
punch in the shoulder.

The Blacksmith standing speaks up.

                    SOLOMON
          The Marshal stepped in
          and stopped the Mayor's
          thugs from hurting me
          and I thank you for that
          but I can't lose my
          shop. How would I feed
          my family then?

He sits and his wife also gives him a
smack and cold shoulder.

Mrs. Trumble stands.

                    MRS. TRUMBLE
          The Marshal helped me
          out too. Thank you
             (beat)
          I don't know what has
          gotten into you men.
          Most of you fought in
          the war and now you're
          acting like frightened
          sheep.

The women of the congregation nod their
heads in agreement.

                    MRS. TRUMBLE
          (CONT'D)
          We need to stand up
          against the Mayor or
          he'll destroy this
          community and we'll have
          no reason to stay... no
          matter how long and hard
          we've worked to build it
          up.

James stands painfully and climbs steps
to be with Melissa.

                    JAMES
          Hello. You all know who
          I am.
            (beat)
          Thomas was my brother.It
          is my responsibility to
          avenge it not yours.

The men nod and elbow their wives as
they agree with James.

                    JAMES (CONT'D)
          But what this corrupt
          Mayor of yours has done
          to you... well, that
          falls on your shoulders
            (beat)
          It might well be that
          the Mayor had something
          to do with my brother's
          death and at that point
                         (MORE)

                         JAMES(CONT'D)
              our purposes cross
              paths. But for your
              family's sakes, for your
              own sense of well being
              you have to stop acting
              like sheep and protect
              what is yours. In 1
              Timothy 5:8 -
                 (beat)
              "But if any provide not
              for his own, and
              specially for those of
              his own house, he hath
              denied the faith, and is
              worse than an infidel."

Melissa's mouth drops a bit at this
surprise bit of biblical knowledge.
James gives her a wink.

The congregation starts to break away
but there is certainly discussion about
what they have just heard. Some walk up
to James and Melissa expressing their
agreement as they depart while others
are stone-faced as they head home.

When the crowd thins a bit James gives
Melissa a soft squeeze on the arm.

                         JAMES
              I'm going over to see my
              brother.

He starts to walk but stumbles a bit.
Melissa helps him stand better and then
offers herself as a crutch to walk to
the grave.

EXT. THOMAS' GRAVE - MORNING

James and Melissa come to a stop at
Thomas's grave. James frees himself
from Melissa's helping hand and
approaches the grave and stops and
looks down at it.

                    JAMES
          Tom. I'm sorry I
          couldn't get here to
          save you... protect you
          like mother always said
          that I should.
             (getting worked up)
          But I stand here right
          now in front of God and
          tell you that I will not
          rest until I have
          destroyed that man, the
          man who killed you and
          all the rest of his
          despicable, Confederate
          pieces of...

Melissa places her hand on James
shoulder

                    MELISSA
          Hush now. This is not
          what Tom would have
          wanted.

                    JAMES
          But I want it. I need
          it.

                    MELISSA
          I know that you are not
          a religious man. How you
          came to know that bible
          verse I'll never know
          but you are an honest
          man, a moral man.

James begins to calm down.

                    MELISSA
          Revenge isn't your job
          James. In Romans it
          says, Beloved, never
          avenge yourselves, but
          leave it to the wrath of
          God, for it is written,
          "Vengeance is mine, I
          will repay, says the
          Lord."

James shoulders collapse as he releases
his hate.

Melissa takes James hand into hers.

                    MELISSA (CONT'D)
          However, here on earth
          your job, Marshal
          McCord, is to administer
          Justice.

Melissa looks into James eyes. They
freeze in near embrace.

EXT. MAYOR'S HOUSE - PORCH - DAY

The Mayor is sitting on a bench with a
book trying to look intelligent.

Reb enters and stops in front of the
Mayor casting a shadow across his book.

                    REB
          What're ya reading there
          your honor?

The Mayor removes his reading glasses
and looks up to Reb squinting from the
sun streaming from his back.

                    MAYOR
          You are blocking my
          light.

Reb mockingly moves.

                    REB
          Sorry boss. So what're
          ya readin?

                    MAYOR
          This? This is a book by
          de Tocqueville,
          Democracy in America.
          You ever hear of it?

                    REB
          Can't say as I have.

                    MAYOR
          It's fascinating. This
          Frenchman traveled the
          country after the
          revolution and wrote
          such marvelous words
          about America.
               (beat)
          I thought that I should
          book up on running a
          country. It doesn't pay
          to be ignorant.

                    REB
          Yeah, so about that...

                    MAYOR
          What?

                    REB
          Ignorance.

                    MAYOR
          Yes, what of it?

                    REB
          That Marshal is just
          plain stupid. Heard he
          tried to get them holy
          rollers to put a stop to
          you once and for all. I
          thought I had warned
          him, put the fear of God

                    REB (CONT'D)
          in him so to speak but I
          guess I was wrong.

                    MAYOR
             (consoling tone)
          It's not your fault Reb.
          The man has been asking
          for trouble ever since
          he arrived.

                    REB
          Can I kill him now?

                    MAYOR
          No. I don't need another
          martyr named McCord. No,
          we shall follow the law.
          Raise your right hand.

Reb looks at the Mayor with a queer
expression.

                    MAYOR
Do you solemnly swear to
fulfill the rightful
duties as sheriff of the
town of Fort Howard?

                    REB
Uhh...

                    MAYOR
Say I do.

                    REB
I do.

                    MAYOR
There. Now you can
arrest him.

                    REB
Charges?

                    MAYOR
As if you care. Be
creative. Have fun. Oh,
and deputize a few of
your men too.
   (beat)
With McCord out of my
hair and away from the
army nothing should
get in our way.
   (beat)
All the weapons are
ready. Now all we need
                    (MORE)

                    MAYOR (CONT'D)
          is the remainder of your
          comrades in arms and we
          can make this official.

                    REB
          They'll be here in time
          as I promised.

                    MAYOR
          Good. Now let's remove
          the last fly from the
          ointment.

EXT. COMMUNITY GARDEN - DAY

James and Melissa stroll hand in hand
through an arbor. Fall is in the air
and the plants have started to turn but
the garden is still a beautiful spot
for such a small town.

They are chatting but we can't hear.

                    JAMES
          ...when the war broke
          out my brother was
          finishing divinity
          school. I had been a US
          marshal for a few years.
          I came home to
          Massachusetts, joined
          the twelfth Mass and
          marched off to fight
          evil.
                         (MORE)

                    JAMES (CONT'D)
          He chose to fight evil
          by heading West and
          preaching words of love
          and forgiveness.
            (beat)
          I thought of him as a
          coward. Running away
          from the hard work of
          keeping the country
          together and putting an
          end to slavery.
            (ashamed)
          Turns out he had one
          heck of a fight right
          here...

                    MELISSA
          We are all called to do
          the Lord's work in
          different ways.

                    JAMES
          As it would appear
            (beat)
          So, we're you and my
          brother close?

                    MELISSA
          As in?

                    JAMES
          Well, you know... Were
          you two... Did he...

> MELISSA
> Are you asking if we
> were courting?
> (giggles)
> Heavens no! We were
> close, yes, but he was
> like an older brother,
> and we had a mutual
> desire to expose the
> Mayor.
> (beat)
> He never asked father
> for his permission and
> he certainly never
> showed any signs of
> interest other than our
> mutual desire to expose
> the Mayor and his
> crimes.
> (beat)
> I suppose now that I
> think on it that Thomas
> may have had some
> designs on me, but,
> don't be offended but
> Tom was not the type of
> man I would want to
> settle down with.

She coyly looks at James.

> MELISSA
> Why do you ask?

> JAMES
> Oh, nothing, just
> curious, um...

> MELISSA
> Tom had a good head on
> his shoulders and all
> and I loved talking with
> him but...

She steps closer to him.

> MELISSA (CONT'D)
> Would you like to have a
> talk with my father...

> JAMES
> (embarrassed)
> Not... Oh! I... uh...
> I'm not...

Reb, Buford, Whitey, Slim, and Lefty
with guns drawn surround James and
Melissa.

James reaches for his gun and Reb stops
his hand from behind and pulls it out
and points it at James.

> REB
> Sorry to break up this
> little... moment. It was
> a moment, right?

> MELISSA
> What are you doing?

                    REB
          It seems that this here,
          law man, is being
          accused of pardon me
          ma'am, rape.

                    JAMES
          What...?

                    REB
          The other night we
          stopped your man here
          from having his way with
          my gal Ginny. But it
          turns out that he did
          more than rough her up.
          She says he did all
          sorts of things that
          even offend my delicate
          ears. And what's even
          worse she confessed to
          me that your preacher
          man behaved the same way
          towards her.
             (beat)
          Imagine, a minster of
          the Lord acting like an
          animal towards another
          mans woman.That's called
          coveting isn't it.

Melissa looks to James in disbelief.
Disbelief in the current situation and
in the accusations.

                    REB
          But, this McCord seems
          to have done more than
          covet.

                    JAMES
          Do not believe him.

                    MELISSA
          I don't.

Reb shows his sheriff's badge.

                    REB
          My deputies and I are
          here to take McCord to
          jail.

Melissa tries to stop them but James
signals not to try. She watches as they
drag him off.

EXT. STREET - DAY

James is tied up and pushed towards the
jail. Melissa walks behind them.

Melissa watches James being dragged
off, the Mayor appears behind her.

                    MAYOR
          It's too bad...

Melissa is startled by the sudden voice
coming from behind her. She stops to
face the Mayor.

                    MAYOR (CONT'D)
          ...but some people's
          true natures are never
          revealed until something
          awful happens.

While Melissa's back is turned. James
is tied to the whipping post. Mayor
sees it, keeps Melissa distracted.

                    MELISSA
          What are you doing? You
          know that the Marshal
          would never do anything
          like this.

James's shirt is removed.

                    MAYOR
          It might be that this is
          a false accusation but
          until there is a
          decision from a judge I
          am obligated to protect
          all the women of this
          town, indeed of the
          entire territory and
          keep a potential threat
          from running loose.

The Mayor steps back and takes an
admiring look at Melissa.

A crowd gathers around James.

                    MAYOR
          You know, you really are
          a remarkably beautiful
          woman.

Melissa is shocked by the tack in the
conversation.

                    MAYOR (CONT'D)
          I don't want to say too
          much, but things are
          about to change around
          here and an ambitious
          man who has risen to the
          top could use a
          beautiful woman such as
          yourself by his side.

                    MELISSA
               (confused)
          What are you saying to
          me?

The henchmen push the crowd back.

                    MAYOR
          I'm saying that this
          territory is about to
          experience a new start
          and I'm going to lead
          it.
               (beat)
          You could be there with
          me.
                              (MORE)

                    MAYOR (CONT'D)
          You could have anything
          you want.

Lefty prepares his bullwhip.

                    MELISSA
          I don't want anything. I
          want you to free James.

The CRACK of the bullwhips first
strike.

Melissa turns. The Mayor grabs her, and
stops her. He holds her close.

                    MAYOR
          James is it? Well, I
          think, if McCord is
          cleared of the rape
          charges, you know we
          hang rapists right?
          Well, maybe then he can
          be freed.
             (beat)
          Certainly not before I
          finish a certain
          business deal... After
          that... and no one gets
          in my way? Perhaps even
          if certain people learn
          to cooperate with me...

The Mayor smiles making sure that she
understands his drift.

Melissa breaks free and turns to see
the second strike of the whip.

                    MAYOR (CONT'D)
          Maybe then the charges
          could be dropped...
            (beat)
          After all he is being
          accused by a known
          prostitute.
            (beat)
          Such a shameful
          profession.

In shock and disbelief Melissa runs
away from the Mayor and towards James.

Ginny is watching too, almost in
disbelief.

Another strike of the bullwhip crosses
James's exposed back.

                    MAYOR (CONT'D)
          She would make such a
          lovely first lady...

Melissa breaks through the line of
henchmen, just as Lefty raises his arm.
She embraces The bloody James from
behind.

INT. GREEN'S CABIN - DAY

Melissa sits at table with Stratton and
Elizabeth. They have been in a series
discussion.

                    MELISSA
          You have to help get
          James out of jail. He
          didn't do anything.

                    STRATTON
          Rape is a mighty serious
          charge...

                    MELISSA
          Father! You know that
          the Mayor is no good.
          Why do you pretend that,
          somehow, he is a
          representative of any
          fair legal system that
          must be obeyed?

                    ELIZABETH
          Now, Melissa, your
          father and I came from a
          place where we trusted
          our leaders and followed
          the laws.

                    STRATTON
          I know how you may feel
          but this thing you ask
          will be dangerous and
          you told us that the
          Mayor did say that James
          would be free after some
          deal he is working on is
          completed.

                    MELISSA
          Father, the deal is
          insurrection. The Mayor
          has a cache of arms
          ready to distribute to
          the group of former
          confederate settlers to
          form an army and
          establish his own
          country. One day soon
          more men will arrive and
          then he figures that he
          will have enough men to
          not be stopped.

                    ELIZABETH
          And what of the army?

                    MELISSA
          He will have enough men
          to overpower the small
          contingent that is here.

                    STRATTON
          But how can getting
          James out of the jail
          stop this, this war?

                    MELISSA
          In the first place the
          Mayor is going to kill
          James no matter what.

                    ELIZABETH
          Why?

                    MELISSA
          For the same reason we
          need him to stop what's
          going on. James is the
          only man who has stood
          up to the Mayor since
          Tom died. And as a US
          Marshal he represents
          the federal government,
          the soldiers will listen
          to him.We can stop the
          Mayor before he can
          carry off his plan.

                    STRATTON
          This sound s so far
          fetched... and he is the
          Mayor.

                    MELISSA
          But father, the Mayor
          was never elected! He
          assumed the position
          when no one else would
          step up to lead the
          community.

Stratton and Elizabeth look to each
other thinking.

                    MELISSA (CONT'D)
          I'm asking you to step
          up now and help me free
          James and put an end to
          the Mayor and all his
                              (MORE)

                    MELISSA (CONT'D)
          evil doings. Therefore
          to him that knoweth to
          do good, and doeth it
          not, to him if is sin.

                    ELIZABETH
          James 4:17.

                    STRATTON
          I always thought that we
          may have educated our
          daughter a little too
          much.

Melissa jumps up and gives her parents
a hug.

                    STRATTON (CONT'D)
          What would you have me
          do?

                    MELISSA
          Go to as many in the
          congregation as you can
          and have them meet here
          tomorrow morning. I
          have an idea that I need
          them to hear me out.

                    ELIZABETH
               (tenderly)
          Is there something else
          going on sweetheart?

Melissa pauses to consider the
question.

                    MELISSA
          Well, yes, I think I've
          fallen in love with
          James.

                    STRATTON
          You know that he's not
          the type to settle down,
          right?

                    MELISSA
          I know father, I know. I
          will face that after
          though. First we have to
          stop the Mayor.

                    STRATTON
          Okay. I'll spread the
          word.

                    MELISSA
          Thank you, I love you
          father.

                    STRATTON
          And I you sweetheart.

Melissa stands and hugs her parents.

EXT. FORT HOWARD - DAY

MONTAGE - Stratton speaks to members of
the congregation

MOS. Stratton asks Blacksmith for help.
Blacksmith shakes his head no. Stratton
pleads but no go.

MOS Stratton asks another man. He
listens. Agrees.

MOS Stratton rides up to a man in a
field. They talk. The man agrees.

MOS Stratton approaches a couple on the
road. Man shakes his head no.

END OF MONTAGE

EXT. GREEN CABIN - MORNING

A group of seven men with their guns
has assembled outside the Greens house.
They mill about chatting. Two more ride
up and dismount. One is the Blacksmith.
Stratton greets him heartily.

Melissa steps out of the house onto the
porch.

                    MELISSA
          Thank you all for
          helping. I know that
          this is asking a lot but
          if we do not succeed in
          breaking the Marshal out
          of jail we risk a bigger
          catastrophe and the end
          to our desire for
          statehood.

                    SOLOMON
          Just what are you
          talking about? I'm here
          because my wife insisted
          but that doesn't mean I
          won't turn around and
          leave if I'm not
          comfortable with this
          whole thing.

                    MELISSA
          Like my father told you.
          The Marshal has been
          jailed under false
          pretenses to keep him
          out of the way of the
          Mayor's big deal.
               (beat)
          What James, Marshal
          McCord discovered is
          that the Mayor, with
          help from former
          Confederate soldiers,
          intends on claiming this
          territory we live in as
          a new republic with him
          as president.

The group talks amongst themselves.

                    MELISSA (CONT'D)
          The Marshal is the one
          man who has the backing
          of the federal troops in
          town and the only man
                              (MORE)

                    MELISSA (CONT'D)
who is willing to take
on the Mayor,
     (beat)
We have enough men right
now to do what needs
doing, however, when the
fighting men the Mayor
has hired arrive we
will be outnumbered,
even counting the
federal troops.
     (beat)
Many of you fought for
the Union in the war. A
couple of you fought for
the South. No matter
your political
differences then, none
of you fought to uphold
a dictator. And the
Mayor intends on
becoming a dictator.

                    SOLOMON
I fought to end
slavery... living under
a dictator would be like
living in slavery with
the Mayor as our owner.
That I am willing to
fight over!

                    STRATTON
          It says in Galatians,
          Stand fast therefore in
          the liberty wherewith
          Christ hath made us
          free, and be not
          entangled again with the
          yoke of bondage.

The gathered men agree. There is
clapping. Shouts of "amen" are heard.

                    MELISSA
          Thank you.
             (beat)
          Now father will go over
          our plan to take over
          the jail and free
          the Marshal. I'm going
          to ride ahead and speak
          to Captain Lewis. Good
          luck.

The men gather closer to Stratton while
Melissa climbs onto her horse. And she
exits.

EXT. JAIL HOUSE - DAY

Stratton slowly rides his horse up to
the small jail house. Slim stands guard
becomes attentive and holds his rifle
at the ready.

Stratton dismounts and unties a cloth
bag from his saddle than approaches the
guard.

                    STRATTON
          My daughter has sent a
          few items for the
          Marshal.

                    SLIM
          What's in the bag?

Stratton opens the bag.

                    STRATTON
          Oh, let's see.

He sets the bag on the porch and starts
removing items.

                    STRATTON (CONT'D)
          Looks like some fried
          chicken...

He holds up a dish covered in a towel.

                    STRATTON (CONT'D)
          And an apple, no two,
          looks like three
          apples...

He sets each one down deliberately.

                    STRATTON (CONT'D)
          And...

INT. JAIL HOUSE - DAY

James is sitting in the single cell
that is located in this very spartan
jail. On the other side of the bars
sits Lefty. Otherwise the room is
empty.

They can hear Stratton as he describes
each of the many items in the bag.

                    STRATTON (O.C.)
          And some boiled eggs...

                    LEFTY
          Sounds like your
          girlfriend has gone and
          brought us some dinner.

                    JAMES
          That's for me.

                    LEFTY
          Sure, we may let you
          suck on some of the
          bones.

                    STRATTON (O.C.)
          Oh, and it looks like
          some apple pie...

                    JAMES
          Her mother makes the
          best apple pie.

Lefty goes over to the door and unlocks
it and opens it a crack to see the
stuff that Stratton has brought.

EXT. JAIL HOUSE - DAY

Slim is focused on the food that seems
to be never ending being pulled from
the sack by Stratton

                    STRATTON
          ...and here's another
          egg.Just how much did
          she stuff in here.

The jail house door opens a crack and
Lefty's face can be seen.

                    SLIM
          Now don't you go and eat
          all that food you hear
          me?

Slim, distracted keeps his focus on the
growing pile of food. Stratton glances
up and sees men from the congregation
slipping along the left and right sides
of the now open jail door. Slim and
Lefty are too distracted to pay
attention.

                    STRATTON
          And, finally...

Stratton pulls out a hand gun and cocks
the hammer and points it at Slim. Lefty
attempts to slam the door shut but the

men have reached the door and force
their way in pushing him back into the
jail house.

INT. JAIL HOUSE - DAY

Lefty is pushed up against the bars of
the cell where James grabs onto him.

EXT. JAIL HOUSE - DAY

Stratton stands pointing his gun at
Slim who drops his rifle and puts his
hands up. Stratton motions for him to
go into the jail house.

EXT. MAYOR'S HOUSE - PORCH - DAY

The Mayor is sitting on his porch
reading one of his books on democracy.
He looks up pour himself a drink. and
sees Stratton pointing his gun at
Buford and walk him into the jail
house.

The Mayor stands in surprise.

Reb comes running up the steps.

         REB
     I was coming out of the
     store and looked across
     the yard and saw those
     farmers take over the
     jail!

                    MAYOR
          Oh I saw them.

                    REB
          This isn't good.

                    MAYOR
          Get the rest of your men
          and stop them before
          they break the Marshal
          out.

                    REB
          That cell is pretty
          solid it will take some
          time to do that.

                    MAYOR
          Well, don't waste any
          more of it get going!

Reb runs off.

The Mayor picks up a gun from the table
and checks it. And then looks to the
jail house. The door is closed and all
looks quiet.

INT. JAIL HOUSE - DAY

                    STRATTON
          Where is the key?

                    LEFTY
          We don't have it...

Stratton points his gun at Buford.

                    STRATTON
          Who does?

                    SLIM
          Reb...

The Solomon opens his bag and pulls out
a hammer and cold chisel.

                    SOLOMON
          Thought these would come
          in handy.

Everyone clears the door and the
Solomon starts to attack the lock.

EXT. ARMY ENCAMPMENT - DAY

Melissa has dismounted from her horse
and approaches the tent of Captain
Lewis. He is seated at a table under
the awning.

CAPTAIN LEWIS

Ah, miss Green. Please sit.

                    MELISSA
          There's no time for
          that. James is in jail.

                    CAPTAIN LEWIS
          Yes, I heard. Pretty
          nasty charges against
          him.

                    MELISSA
          False charges. The Mayor
          arrested him to keep him
          out of the way. Right
          now my father and a few
          of the men from the
          church are breaking him
          out of jail. I need your
          help.

                    CAPTAIN LEWIS
          I can't interfere with
          local civil laws. It's
          illegal...

INT.   JAIL HOUSE - DAY

The Solomon gives the hammer one final
swing and the lock breaks and the door
swings open.

The thugs are tied up and sitting on
the floor against the wall.

                    JAMES
          Okay, now let's get out
          of here.

Stratton opens the jail house door and
a shot glances off the door frame. He
quickly closes the door and the men
become concerned.

                    JAMES (CONT'D)|
          Looks like they know
          what we're up to.

James grabs the thug's rifle.

                    JAMES (CONT'D)
          Well, if we stay in here
          we're trapped. I'll
          make a run for it and
          draw their fire.

                    STRATTON
          Stop. What are you
          looking to do son?

                    JAMES
          Looking for a miracle.
          Say a prayer for me.

James stands by the side of the door
getting ready to charge out into the
fun fire.

EXT. ARMY ENCAMPMENT - DAY

GUN FIRE is heard coming from the
direction of the jail house.

Melissa looks in that direction of the
sound.

                    MELISSA
          Oh no! They got caught.
          Please...

                    CAPTAIN LEWIS
          I told Marshal McCord
          that my hands are tied
          when it comes to
                              (MORE)

                    CAPTAIN LEWIS
               (CONT'D)
               interference in civil
               law. But this sounds
               like a revolution is
               taking place.
                    (smiles)
               This is something I can
               handle. Let's go!

EXT. JAIL HOUSE - DAY

The jail house door creeps open. The
door is peppered with gun fire. Door
closes quickly.

Reb and a few of his men are positioned
around the jail house though there is
only one door.

                    REB
               (to his men)
               Nobody shoots the
               Marshal... He's mine!

The door opens again and again the Reb
and his men riddle the opening with gun
fire.

INT. JAIL HOUSE - DAY

There is gun fire and James slams the
door closed.

                    JAMES
          Looks like the Lord
          hasn't jammed their
          guns.

                    STRATTON
            (smiles)
          That's not quite His
          way.

                    JAMES
          Obviously.

James thinks for a bit. He looks around
the room. He sees that there are no
windows and no other doors. He looks at
the thugs tied up on the floor. And
then he looks at the men who risked
their lives to rescue him.

                    JAMES (CONT'D)
          Hand me that white towel
          over there.

James tears it a few times.

                    STRATTON
          What are you going to
          do?

                    JAMES
          Those men don't want you
          and I don't want you to
          die because of me.

James ties the towel to the barrel of
the rifle.

Stratton looks at the white flag.

                    STRATTON
          So you're going to
          surrender?

James holds up the flag.

                    JAMES
          No, just making a
          strategic maneuver.

Stratton looks at him quizzically.

                    JAMES (CONT'D)
          Buy some time for that
          miracle.

James stands by the door.

                    JAMES
               (to Stratton)
          What did I say about
          praying?

James smiles at the men he turns and
opens the door and pokes the flag out
the crack.

EXT. JAIL HOUSE - DAY

The door opens and the gun fire erupts
again. A white flag pokes out the
opening.

                    REB
          (to his men)
          Hold your damned fire!

Reb cautiously stands pointing his gun
in the direction of the flag and he
calls out to the jail house.

                    REB (CONT'D)
          Come on out of there! No
          one will shoot.

James makes a slow hesitant move out
the door. Once on the porch the door
closes shut behind him. James takes
several steps towards Reb.

                    REB (CONT'D)
          That's good McCord! What
          do you want?

                    JAMES
          Would you hanging from a
          gallows be possible?

                    REB
          For a Yankee whose about
          to get shot you're a
          funny man.

Reb raises his rifle and aims at James.

                        REB (CONT'D)
                   Sorry we don't have more
                   time for a longer
                   conversation but you
                   have an appointment with
                   your brother.

Reb cocks the hammer on his repeating
rifle and his finger starts to pull
back on the trigger.

James stares him down unafraid.

The sound of a shot rings out. James
remains standing.

Reb has been shot in the arm and he is
on the ground. Behind him is Captain
Lewis with Melissa and several of his
men. Captain Lewis is lowering his
rifle having just shot Reb. He signals
for his men to round up the rest of the
henchmen.

Melissa runs to James and the men come
out of the jail house.

EXT. MAYOR'S HOUSE - PORCH - DAY

The Mayor has been watching the action
from his porch. He sees that things are
unraveling. Before anyone comes for him
he heads out the other side mounts a
horse and makes for an escape through
the town gate.

EXT. JAIL HOUSE - DAY

Melissa and the men are gathered
together in a celebration of relief.

                    STRATTON
          When you call for a
          miracle...

                    JAMES
          Wouldn't have happened
          without that prayer.

Stratton gives a sheepish look.

                    JAMES (CONT'D)
          You did pray, right?

                    STRATTON
          I, I was too afraid that
          you'd be shot when you
          stepped onto the porch.
          I guess I was
          distracted.

                    JAMES
          Perhaps the prayer was
          always there in your
          heart...

                    SOLOMON
          Hey! There goes the
          Mayor out the gate!

Without much hesitation James stuffs a
couple hand guns in his belt and picks

up a rifle then climbs on a horse. He
looks to Melissa.

                    JAMES
          You know where I'm
          headed. Gotta go!

James says no more and rides out after
the Mayor.

                    CAPTAIN LEWIS
          Where's he going?

Melissa removes the map from her coat
opens it and stabs a finger where the
hide out is.

EXT. TRAPPERS FORT - DAY

The Mayor pulls up his horse outside
the overgrown trapper stockade which he
uses for his cache of stolen goods and
weapons stash. He dismounts, ties up
his horse and runs inside the stockade.

I/E. TRAPPERS FORT - DAY

The Mayor rushes through the gate and
into the small interior yard of the
stockade which is piles with barrels
and crates of various kinds. There are
a couple loose bags which he grabs and
proceeds to a door of one of the
cabins.

EXT. TRAPPERS FORT - DAY

James rides up to the trappers
stockade. He sees the Mayors horse then
notices that the gate is pushed open.
He dismounts and draws one of the guns
from his belt. And proceeds with
caution through the gates.

INT. TRAPPERS FORT - CABIN - DAY

The Mayor is inside a cabin that is
full of stolen loot. He lights a
lantern so the room can be illuminated.
He opens boxes of various kinds and
starts filling the bags with gold
coins, paper currency, jewelry and
other stolen treasures. In his haste he
knock over a strong box that crashes to
the ground generating a loud noise.

INT. TRAPPERS FORT - YARD - DAY

James looks around the yard wary that
the Mayor might be hiding behind some
of the barrels and crates waiting to
ambush him. He surveys the cabin doors
and as he sees the open one there is a
loud crashing sound that comes out of
it.

He hurries over to the open door and
plants himself behind some crates.

INT. TRAPPERS FORT - CABIN - DAY

The Mayor kicks the fallen box out of
his way and continues to fill his bags.

                    JAMES (O.S.)
          Hey! Mayor. I've kind a
          got you boxed in. Why
          don't you just come on
          out of there with your
          hands where I can see
          them and we'll end this
          thing...

Mayor stops filling the bags and draws
his gun. He pears out the small window
and scans the yard outside. He sees
nothing then he hears...

                    JAMES (O.S.)
          Come on! Your finished!
          Just give it up!

The Mayor looks in the direction of the
voice and sees James crouched behind
crates. He takes aim and fires.

INT. TRAPPERS FORT - YARD - DAY

The shots fired from the cabin pepper
the crate that James is hiding behind.
He ducks, repositions himself and
returns fire.

A gun fight ensues. The Mayor firing at
James and missing while James returns

fire and misses. Then the firing stops
from inside the cabin.

James rushes the door and charges
inside.

INT. TRAPPERS FORT CABIN - DAY

The Mayor is reloading when James
barges into the cabin. He has no time
to react and James tackles him to the
ground. Then James stands and brings
his gun to bare on the Mayor.

>   MAYOR
> What? You're going to
> shoot? This is mercy?

>   JAMES
> I'm not the preacher, my
> brother was.

>   MAYOR
> Please! I surrender. But
> don't shoot! I'm not
> ready to die...

>   JAMES
> But Thomas was?

>   MAYOR
> It was Reb! I told him
> not to but...

James lowers his gun just a bit. The
Mayor takes that as a sign to act. He

grabs some debris from the floor and
throws it into James face.

James staggers back from the stuff in
his eyes.

The Mayor springs to his feet and grabs
a bag of loot. He almost gets around
James who grabs him and pulls him to
the ground where he proceeds to beat
the stuffing out of the Mayor.

EXT. TRAPPERS FORT - DAY

Melissa and Captain Lewis ride up to
the stockade and dismount. Captain
lewis, who is armed, leads the way
through the gate.

INT. TRAPPERS FORT - YARD - DAY

Melissa and Captain Lewis look around
the yard at the pile of barrels and
crates.

The noise of the fight flows out of the
open cabin door and they rush to it.

INT. TRAPPERS FORT- CABIN - CONTINOUS
- DAY

Melissa and Captain Lewis stand in the
open doorway of the cabin and see James
mercilessly beating the Mayor to death
with his bare hands.

Captain Lewis pulls James off the Mayor
then keeps his gun trained on him

Melissa pulls James to the side and
tries to calm him down.

                    MELISSA
          James, Tom would not
          want you to kill this
          man.

James is in a froth and needs further
calming.

                    MELISSA (CONT'D)
          The Lord tells us; For
          all have sinned, and
          come short of the glory
          of God.

James appears to respond to the bible
quote and visibly calms down.

Captain Lewis drags the Mayor out of
the cabin and stands him before James
in the open.

                    MAYOR
          You know Marshal, you
          come here all mighty
          with your federal laws
          thinking you know what
          for and where of but did
          you know that your
          brother and your
                    (MORE)

                    MAYOR (CONT'D)
          girlfriend here were
          seeing each other in a
          sinful manner?

Melissa is shocked.

                    MAYOR (CONT'D)
          And that he was cheating
          on her besides.

                    MELISSA
          You shut up! Do not
          listen to him James.

                    MAYOR
          Oh, yes, they were the
          scandal of the town but
          no one spoke of it...

James steam starts to boil up again. He
raises his gun and cocks the hammer and
points it at the Mayor's head finger on
the trigger.

                    MAYOR (CONT'D)
          Captain! you can't let
          him do this! I'm a
          prisoner...

                    CAPTAIN LEWIS
          Not sure I much care
          what you are or aren't
          at this point.

James holds the gun inches from the
Mayor's forehead. The gun shakes in his
hand, he is ready to shoot.

Melissa places her hand on James
shoulder and he drops the gun to his
side and he breaks. They hug.

The Mayor senses the Captains guard
drop and breaks free he runs for the
cabin door across the yard and slams
the door closed.

                    CAPTAIN LEWIS
          (CONT'D)
          Oh, damn!

                    JAMES
            (snapped out of his
          funk)
          Not your fault, I let my
          emotions get in the way
          but he's still trapped.

INT. TRAPPERS FORT - CABIN - DAY

The Mayor barricades the door closed.
He is in the dark. He lights a match
and finds a lantern which he lights.
The interior of this cabin is full of
crates of rifles, ammo and gun powder.
He pulls out one of the repeating
rifles and quickly loads it then heads
to the small window and looks out.

                    MAYOR
          (yelling out the window)
          Let's just say I let you
          keep all that's left
          here in the stockade and
          you let me ride out with
          the bags of money and
          we'll call it even.

INT. TRAPPERS FORT - CABIN - CONTINOUS
- DAY

                    JAMES
          We're not even until you
          pay for your crimes and
          Thomas's death.

Mayor inside the cabin.

                    MAYOR
          I just offered you
          payment. How much more
          do you want?

                    JAMES
          Justice.

A shot rings out from the window and
nearly hits James. The three duck
behind crates.

The Mayor continues to fire. The rifle
jams, he pulls out his revolver.

Captain Lewis looks to James and James
gives him a nod. Together they open up

and shoot into the open window the
Mayor had been standing in.

INT. TRAPPERS FORT - CABIN - CONTINOUS
- DAY

The spray of gun fire into the window
opening cause the Mayor to fall back
into the cabin. The Mayor repositions
himself, he has a clear shot of James,
he pulls up his revolver with both
hands in aims it and fires.

The old gun blows up in the Mayors
face. He falls back and knocks over the
light lantern, and fire quickly
spreads. He's blinded, he staggers
around trying to wipe his eyes clean.

The fire flares up and the room is
fully illuminated showing stacks of
guns and barrels of powder and crates
of TNT.

                    MAYOR
          Oh no!

The Mayor stomps at the flames for a
moment but realizes that is a lost
cause and the flames like the sides of
the barrels and crates.

He goes to the door and desperately
tries to remove the barricade.

INT. TRAPPERS FORT - YARD - DAY

                    MAYOR (O.S.)
              Help! You gotta help me!

James goes to the door and tries to
push it open.

A round of ammo cooks off, then another
and then several more.

Captain Lewis pulls James away from the
door.

                    CAPTAIN LEWIS
              We have to get out of
              here!

                    MAYOR (O.S.)
                 (yells)
              H E L P!

The fire becomes visible licking out
the small window. The Mayor's screams
for help become pathetic.

                    MAYOR (O.S.)
                 (CONT'D)
              Dear God in heaven...

A powder keg explodes and the row of
cabins is consumed in flames.

EXT. TRAPPERS FORT - DAY

James, Melissa and Captain Lewis flee
the stockade and drag the horses away

to a safe distance where they watch the
stockade burn.

Melissa hugs James as he watches the
the old stockade go up in flames.

                    JAMES
          Well, I guess that's the
          end of the insurrection.
            (to Captain Lewis)
          Thanks for your help
          Captain.

                    CAPTAIN LEWIS
          No, thank you. Without
          your discovering the
          plot we would have been
          over taken and the Mayor
          would have established
          his own private country.
          It would have meant
          another war. He would
          have lost, of course,
          but I have grown weary
          of killing.

Melissa watches the fire.

                    MELISSA
          Then said Jesus unto
          him, put up again thy
          sword into his place:
          for all they that take
          the sword shall perish
          with the sword.

                    JAMES
          Amen to that.
            (beat)
          I think we should get
          back and make sure the
          rest of the scum are
          taken care of.

The three mount their horses and ride
back to town.

EXT. ORCHARD/BURNED CHURCH - LATER- DAY

James, Melissa, and Captain Lewis on
their horses have stopped at the church
ruins.

The cross foundation looks very weak,
the cross appears to be titling down
forward, they don't notice.

James dismounts.

                    JAMES
          There's something I got
          to do.

                    MELISSA
          I'll join you.

                    CAPTAIN LEWIS
          I'm continuing back to
          the town.

Captain Lewis rides off.

James assists Melissa dismount. He
holds her around the waist, facing him
they look into each other eyes. They
are about to kiss.

Reb appears from behind the ruins. With
his gun drawn on them.

                    REB
          Did I interrupt you two,
          again?

Before James can go for his gun.

                    REB (CONT'D)
          Don't even think about
          it.

James puts himself in front of Melissa.

                    REB (CONT'D)
          You two make quite the
          couple. You both kill
          the Mayor and claimed
          the loot for yourselves?

                    JAMES
          The place exploded. He
          died in the fire.

                    REB
          A fire. What do they
          call that?
              (beat)
          On, yeah, irony.

                    JAMES
          The loot you say, will
          be recovered by the
          proper authorities.

The cross's foundation continues to
crumble, the cross tilts down toward
Reb.

                    REB
          NO. It's all mine now,
          but first I got to kill
          you both, right where I
          killed the reverend.
          That's what I call
          irony.

Reb takes aim at James.

CRACK, the large heavy cross falls down
onto Reb's head. Then CRASH, Reb is
crushed.

EXT. JAIL HOUSE - LATER - DAY

James, and Melissa ride up in front of
the jail house. Reb's body lays across
James horse. Captain Lewis and an armed
guard made up of soldiers and Stratton
and men from the congregation stand
circling the Mayor's henchmen, Slim,
Buford, Whitey, and Lefty are sitting
on the ground.

Many of the towns people, including
Ginny are there.

Buford has a sloppy field dressing
covering his shot up arm. He stands and
tries to approach James but is blocked
by men with guns.

                    BUFORD
          The Marshall killed the
          Mayor and Reb.

James takes the challenge and
approaches Reb.

                    JAMES
          No. Their actions did
          that.

One of the Soldiers grabs Buford, and
sits him down.

Captain Lewis approaches.

                    JAMES (CONT'D)
               (to Captain Lewis)
          Can your men watch these
          prisoners until I get
          back from San Francisco
          with a few more
          Marshals?

                    CAPTAIN LEWIS
          We're not going
          anywhere. But don't
          dawdle... And don't you
          dare leave this mess for
          me to sort out.

                    JAMES
          Captain? Why would you
          ever think that I might
          just decide to keep on
          riding and not look
          back.

They both look down at the henchmen.

                    CAPTAIN LEWIS
          Well, maybe I wouldn't
          blame you too much if
          you did.

Captain Lewis turns and supervises his
troops as they stand each of the
henchmen and lead them into the jail
house.

James, Melissa and Stratton turn and
walk for their horses.

EXT. BURNED OUT CHURCH/GRAVE - MORNING

James rides up to the church. His horse
is loaded with his bed roll, sack of
food and other items for the long ride
ahead. He dismounts and walks to the
grave of his brother and kneels on one
knee.

                    JAMES
          Well, Tommy I'm not
          quite done with
          things... Never could be
                    (MORE)

                    JAMES (CONT'D)
          unless I could bring you
          back...

He hears a noise coming from behind him
and quickly turns drawing his gun.

                    JAMES (CONT'D)
          I'm sure you know how
          sneaking up behind
          someone can be bad for
          your health.

                    MELISSA
          And I'm sure the you
          don't know that riding
          away without say good
          bye can be bad for
          yours.

Melissa approaches James as he stands.
They face gazing into each other's eyes
then embrace and kiss.

                    MELISSA (CONT'D)
          Will you be returning?

                    JAMES
          Yes, with more marshals
          who will the prisoners.

                    MELISSA
          That isn't what I
          meant...

                    JAMES
               (softly)
          I know.

                    MELISSA
          Then will you?

                    JAMES
          Yes, I'll stay. I hear
          the position of Sheriff
          is open.

They embrace again, kiss and embrace
holding the moment as the camera pulls
out, as the sun sets.

                         FADE OUT

I hope you enjoyed my workbook. I wish you good luck with your adventures.

Send your questions to dcrahe.com